What those who should know, have to say about this book:

"Spanking good fun! Informative, entertaining and practical! Andrea Fitting zippingly explains why and how to brand your business. Her insider view of brands like Cutco, Southwest Airlines and Luna Bars are genius. It's a fast, fun read, written by an obvious industry expert."

Barb Moore, former CEO Anderson Transfer; small business consultant

"What Andrea has created in a delightful and witty format is actually a manifesto for all who challenge clichés, mediocrity, and the timidity of those who surround the true Challengers. This is a handbook to be carried around and consulted when you're faced with a client, a colleague, or a boss who just doesn't get it. Andrea has managed to capture the essence of our work and provided a reference guide that will summon the inner Challenger in us all. Each chapter is a carefully crafted "lesson" from a true professional that's been there and spanked it."

Andrea Sardone, Chief Marketing Officer
College of William & Mary School of Business

D1522740

Andrea F. Fitting

ISBN: 098580260X
ISBN-13: 978-0985802608

Apropos Media
Pittsburgh, PA

Cover design by Adam Wilson

Does Your Brand Need a Spanking?

Move Your Brand from Bashful to Badass

By
Andrea F. Fitting, Ph.D.

With
Jason Bittel

Apropos Media
Pittsburgh, PA

Andrea F. Fitting

To Jeff
Who takes my black and white ideas
And turns them into technicolor reality

Andrea F. Fitting

Introduction

Andrea F. Fitting

This Book May Not Be Right For You

Maybe you work for an intractable corporation, one where people say, "the way we've always done it" as though it's a solution and not a problem. Maybe your company is flush with business, you're a market leader and everybody presumes it will just always be this way. Or maybe you're a coward.

Look, I'm not trying to be antagonistic – ok, maybe a little – but one of the tenets of successful branding is that no brand is for everyone. Not Apple, not Nike, not Southwest Airlines. And certainly not Brand Spanking. You can appreciate that.

Plain and simple, there are plenty of people, businesses and brands out there that don't need, don't want or can't handle what I have to say. It's cool. I wish them well. If you're one of them, you can put this book down and go on with your business. No hard feelings.

Still here? Good. I'll let you in on a little secret. Just between us, all those people up there… They're your competition, your Goliath, your industry's 800-pound gorilla. And I don't wish them well. I wish *you* well – you and all the other upstarts, underdogs and rule-breakers. The Goliaths of this world have plenty of other people rooting for them; that's how they've grown so fat and happy. This book is not for them.

This book is for Challenger Brands – brands that are not the market leader in their industries, but think

9

they deserve to be and might actually have a crack at it. Some of the most successful brands on the market were once Challengers. When they were young, fresh and innovative, they shook their industries to the core and made us think differently about what we buy and how we buy it. They are hardly recognizable now as nothing but the bright idea and guts they once were. Among them are the giants of today: Kraft, Kellogg's, Microsoft and Target.

People forget, but Apple Computer was a Challenger Brand when IBM was the market leader. In those days no one but Apple imagined it was possible to have an affordable personal computer for work, not just a "dumb terminal" on your desktop connected to a room-sized mainframe. Toyota was a Challenger Brand when American cars were the standard of excellence and luxury and American consumers thought of things made in Japan as cheap and second rate. MySpace dominated the social network when Facebook was but a blinking pixel in Mark Zuckerberg's eye.

Often, we don't even realize how much of a Challenger some companies still are. Method has only a small slice of the cleaning products pie compared to Procter & Gamble. Whole Foods is not nearly as ubiquitous as Kroger or Safeway or Publix, but it has managed to change the way we think about the grocery category.

Challenger Brands come in a variety of flavors. There are the kind that break onto the scene with an entirely new concept and invent a category, like

Groupon. There are the kind that sell something as common as books in an entirely new way, like Amazon. Some see an opportunity and a need to deliver a service using technology that wasn't possible before, such as eTrade. And some start out with a mission to do well by doing good – a social entrepreneurship calling – like TOMS Shoes.

We need to pay attention to Challenger Brands and take them seriously. Even the ones that will never become the largest companies in their industries have something important to teach us. They often change the way we think about their categories, and sometimes the world, forever. These companies are run by smart, energetic people on a mission. They are thought leaders: clear-thinking people who don't mind taking risks when they see something that could make our lives better. And they bet it all that we'll eventually think so, too. (I call them Firebrands. More on them in a bit.)

This is a book about Challenger Brand owners getting it right.

It's about aligning your brand with the values, policies and messages that actually mean something to your ideal customers. It's about consistency – putting a stake in the ground. Companies that attempt to change their brand messaging or processes because they are uncertain, lack confidence or never really had a clear differentiating value proposition in the first place lose credibility, lose integrity and drive employees and customers right into the arms of the competition. I know - I've seen it happen.

Let's also talk about what this book is not. It is not a How-To for branding – not every reader will have the same issues or obstacles to overcome. You will not read this book – or make your employees read this book – and wake up to a successful brand.

This is not a cookbook – a bulleted list of recipe steps that, when followed, coagulate into the perfect brand. If that's what you're looking for, if you seek the "Joy of Branding" – some sort of tried and true chemistry or algorithm – keep looking. I don't happen to believe that there is such a thing as a perfect brand. No, not even Apple. Even it must evolve to stay relevant and beloved.

Look, I've learned some immutable facts about branding over the last 20-some years. This book is an attempt to share them with you. It contains no magic bullets, formulas or spells – because such things do not exist.

And let's be honest. Branding is dirty, difficult and often thankless work. But when it's done right – with intelligence and passion and commitment – branding becomes an elemental force. It influences decisions and alters perception. Devout followers defend their brands with Capulet/Montague-like fury.

Think I'm wrong? Get a group of people together and ask them who has a better burrito – Chipotle, Moe's or Qdoba. Watch how a debate between iPhones and Droids turns nearly religious. Try to tell your neighbor Bud Light is better than Miller Lite. (Actually, if you're in Pittsburgh, it's probably best that you just order an I.C. Light and keep your mouth shut.)

Burritos, cell phones and nearly indistinguishable, tasteless beers – friendships have been lost over less. And the point is, whether you're selling wrenches, mobile apps, construction consultation or cheddar cheese, you want your customers to behave this way. You want them willing to throw down when someone says there's a better three-ring binder on the market. You won't get them to do that by lowering your cost per unit or offering a new color. This sort of attachment is visceral. Part of it comes from hard and fast brain science, part of it from smoke and steam.

But if you're not learning how to harness it – if you or your superiors "don't believe in branding" – may the gods have mercy.

Because being a Challenger Brand is a way of life. It's an ethos. It's a fracas with the elements. And more brands are engaged in it than they realize.

Andrea F. Fitting

The Night Before Brand Spanking®

It was 4 PM and Belinda, my right hand woman and VP of my agency, came into the office to report that LAMAR, the billboard company, would be posting our new outdoor ad tonight. Brandee would be in 15 prime locations around the city, ready for rush hour traffic – in all her glory. My stomach felt hollow with equal parts anxiety and anticipation.

"Brandee" is what we had decided to call our dominatrix – the icon that would come to symbolize our agency point of view.

Brandee takes no guff. Her M.O. is to tell it like it is. If they – our potential clients – don't like what they hear, they can remain right where they are. She reminds me to lead by example – to go forth fearlessly with our marketing messages and let the world know exactly what they can expect from us.

You see, brand symbols, like flags, are created as much for rallying the internal troops as they are for waving the brand in front of would-be customers and striking fear and discouragement in the hearts of would-be competitors.

Thus far, we'd adopted Brandee and her ways internally. We went to work each morning with a snap in our step, the symbolic whip in hand, but this was something altogether different. This was letting it all hang out.

15

This was the moment I'd been planning and hoping for – the breakthrough – the signal that we were ready to transition from tiny, obscure, one-of-the-pack little boutique creative services agencies – to *WOW, who is that? We want HER on our team!*

Step 1: Get attention and win the opportunity to prove our mettle. This was about walking the walk. For years, we had told our clients to be bold. Be gutsy. State your values and tattoo them on your foreheads. Now it was our turn.

Brandee would be a lightning rod; I knew that much for certain. You can't plaster a 40 x 60 ft dominatrix around a town like Pittsburgh without turning a few heads. Not only would she attract the attention of would-be clients, but she would also raise the ire of the local Puritans who wouldn't get the joke and take offense at the use of innuendo in our advertising.

Problem was, I had no way to know the ratio of good to bad. You never do when you're the first. My gut told me that many people would be at the extremes. Some would be amused, some confused, but in any event, the people who mattered to me, our would-be clients, would feel positive or at least curious about our ad. I guessed that there would be a small minority of those who felt negative, maybe even vehemently so, but only a handful of them would actually speak up about it.
Nevertheless, I tossed and turned all night wondering if I had taken too much of a gamble and made the biggest mistake of my life. What if there

was a major protest and lots of bad press? What if we got picketed by nuns? What if all of our conservative clients, like our law firms, our healthcare systems and our financial services advisors, bailed on us and left us en masse?

In my moments of bravado, I told myself that this was absolutely the right thing to do. I told myself that if all those worst case scenarios happened, I'd just pick myself up and start over. I imagined that the attention and new business we'd win as a result of the Brandee billboards would more than compensate for the losses. I convinced myself that Brandee was the appropriate, well, "face" of the firm I was trying to build – a Challenger: fearless, risk taking, confident and creative. That having a leather-clad dominatrix wielding a whip as our signature icon would help attract exactly the type of client we wanted and ward off those who would waste our time and never, ever take our advice or use our most creative ideas. It was time for us to quit playing by the market leader's rules, quit being conventional and just do what we knew to be right.

But then my stomach knotted up. It was 2002 and my husband had quit his corporate job and joined my agency two years before. All our eggs were in this basket. We had one daughter in college and another about to graduate high school.

Six short months ago, we'd lost the biggest client we'd ever had and we were still reeling. It was terrifying but empowering – failure simply not an option.

17

Looking back now at that night of cold sweats and wild dreams, I can see that it took me entirely too long to make that move. I could have gotten there so much earlier if I'd had the kind of advice I'm about to share with you here.

Book 1: Brand

Andrea F. Fitting

"How's Business?"

Now there's a question you either love or you hate. Whether it's your friend being polite, your father-in-law landing a jab or an industry peer needling for intel – that question can make you squirm like an ant under a magnifying glass.

Maybe business isn't necessarily *bad*. Work is mostly steady, you're keeping things slightly in the black, and the plates you're spinning are not falling too often. Generally speaking, there's nothing you can point to that is a crisis in the making. You're not breaking any records, but that's OK. You work just hard enough to keep things on an even keel.

Except, occasionally there's this feeling that you could be doing much better. (You're reading this book, aren't you?)

Maybe you know deep down (and maybe not so deep) that you aren't really giving it your all anymore and, as a matter fact, neither are your employees. They sense that your enthusiasm is not what it should be and if the boss doesn't seem excited or motivated, why should they bust their asses if you don't expect it of them – or of yourself?

If you've been selling the same stuff, day in and day out, in the same way, it's no wonder you feel lackluster. If each day you come to work and do what you've always done, the way you've always

21

done it, maybe the way your father did it before you... inertia is inevitable. Hell, given the laws of physics, it's natural.

Then something happens. Something big.

Something Big

Maybe it's something personal and highly stressful like a death in the family or your spouse losing his job. Or maybe it's something global that makes you re-evaluate your whole worldview.

That's how it was with us. On September 12th, 2001, this nation collectively sucked in its breath and business as usual was anything but. For the next couple of years, there was a tremendous amount of uncertainty and it showed in the way people behaved.

Virtually no business got away unscathed. Advertising especially came to be viewed as vulgar. Because let's face it, who wants a razor blade or cheese cracker company trying to convince you that their products are of vital importance in your life? Everything seemed completely trivial in the face of such national trauma.

Instead, most companies used their air time or print ad space to send messages of condolences or comfort or national pride. Every corporation and Mom & Pop shop waved the stars and stripes in their windows and on their websites. Every politician donned a flag lapel pin.

And though our government launched a couple of wars and our country began sacrificing its treasure and the lives of our soldiers, most of the rest of us fell into complacency once again. That is until 2008, when the economy collapsed. Today, we are still feeling those ripples and it may yet be a long time before we experience the kind of prosperity most of us came to know.

World events and business cycles like this make it crystal clear why brands are important. Even in the worst economic times, like the Great Depression in the 1930s, consumers still consume – they just consume less. Maybe a lot less. When the pie shrinks, strong brands survive and even thrive, getting the tastiest bites, while weak ones suffer, fighting over the crumbs or starving to death.

Which will you be?

When the Going Gets Tough

Times of trouble should be considered an opportunity for Challenger Brands, a chance to enter markets previously too difficult to penetrate. And that's not just propaganda. You can look through the doldrums of history and see which iconic brands took the opportunity to launch or grow.

- General Electric was established in 1876 by Thomas Edison in the middle of the Panic of 1873, a six-year recession.
- Plymouth, launched as a separate brand in 1928, was Chrysler's first foray into the low-priced market. Plymouth became one of the Great Depression's only successful car brands. (Though, full disclosure, the brand is no longer.)
- Kraft's Miracle Whip, a lower-priced altern-ative to mayonnaise, also was an instant hit in the 1930s.
- FedEx Corp. began operations on April 17, 1973, a time of hyperinflation caused by the oil crisis instigated by OPEC.
- MTV Networks brought innovation and excitement to the music scene when it debuted in the economic slump of 1981.
- Apple launched the iPod only one and a half months after September 11, 2001.

Adversity Can Be Useful

Challenger Brands that have a culture of looking for opportunities to forge ahead will thrive in a crisis. They will see a need and figure out how to shape their products or services to fill it. Brands that have been resting on their haunches when a catastrophe hits will be caught off guard and may go down for the count.

People are resilient. And so are good brands.

When times begin to get tough, there is no mystery about whether or not your brand needs a Spanking – it will be patently obvious. Conversely, when external factors are not bearing down on you or your company and you just feel a malaise but can't exactly say why, that's the time to take a good hard look at whether a Spanking is in order.

What is Brand Spanking?

Brand Spanking is the tough love approach my agency, Fitting Group, takes to turn your brand into the business-generating machine it should and could be. Brand Spanking allows us to crawl inside your brand and extract its key components, then devise a strategy for tactics, messaging, policy and decision-making.

It's an intense process. Questions are asked. Things are said. No quarter is given. And when it's done right, it stings like hell.

But our clients thank us for it. This book is designed to give you a little taste, an at-home preview of the thinking that has to happen for a brand to reach its full potential.

Skeptical? Not even sure if you're really a Challenger Brand? Well, not with that attitude you're not.

Every Brand Needs a Spanking Now and Then

Brand Spanking keeps us disciplined and focused. It keeps us competitive. Spanking your brand is akin to reviewing and improving your messages and how well understood they are both within your company and externally in the marketplace. It's a constant process of asking your customers what they think, observing how they behave, refining your offerings, defining your messages, differentiating through marketing and distribution and following through on the promises you make.

Failing to spank your brand is like inviting competitors to eat you alive. Brands that reach a certain level of success and then linger there, expecting to maintain, will undoubtedly be caught off guard.

Would-be Challengers, hear me: no matter how big your competitors, no matter how dominating, change is absolute. Changes in fashion, trends, economic conditions and technology – all are opportunities for the young upstart brands with nothing to lose.

Market Leaders, We're Coming For You

There's nothing more vulnerable than a coasting market leader. They're the biggest or the best and they think they always will be.

But they're wrong. Change is inevitable. It's a universal force. If you're a market leader who wants to stay there, you must resist the urge to hit cruise control. There are hundreds of brands tired of living in your wake. And they are coming for you.

To head them off at the pass, you need to think like a Challenger Brand: keep moving, keep improving. And keep the covenant you originally made with your customers when you were a young brand – the one that helped you become the market leader.

Brands resting on their laurels send a message to customers that says, "We have you now so we don't have to try any more. We can just keep selling you the same stale stuff in the same old unimaginative way and you'll keep on buying because you clearly don't have any imagination, either."

The Ketchup Bottle

In 2007 alone, 176 million bottles of ketchup were sold in the US. If you're a numbers geek, this amounts to 329.8 million pounds of the stuff. And this doesn't take into account all the ketchup packets consumed with billions of fast-food meals. In other words, people are clearly hitting the sauce both at home and on the go.

Heinz dominates the ketchup market with about a 61% share. (Hunts trails with about 16%, Del Monte with about 5% and the remaining 18% is divided among private label brands.) The product has remained virtually unchanged since its original introduction at the Philadelphia Fair in 1876. So what does Heinz do now to differentiate and justify its premium price? How can it retain the perception of the premium brand among its competitors?

One revolutionary accomplishment was to grasp and then respond to the consumer's biggest complaint about the product. The complaint didn't have anything to do with the red gooey stuff per se. It had to do with the convenience, or lack thereof, of the speed and ease of extracting it from the bottle.

So in 2001, Heinz introduced the "Easy Squeeze" bottle, which is stored cap down and allows the product to flow readily when the soft plastic bottle is squeezed. (Almost simultaneously with Hunt's, I might add.) The consumer-driven innovation resulted in a 17% jump in sales in the first year. This is also a really good argument for why the market leader should always be thinking like a Challenger – always keeping the competition on their toes and giving even your most loyal customers new and better reasons to love you.

Note that Heinz, while introducing a technologically new package, retained most, if not all, of its brand equities and icons – the look, shape, and labeling of its bottle. The consumer draws comfort from the subliminal message that, while the company is being responsive to needs, it is still the same beloved brand "inside." Heinz understands that the visual expression of its brand is an extremely important symbol of its predictability. Because after almost 150 years, people will notice even a small change.

Don't believe me? Think about the Heinz customers in your life. Would they ever condescend to buy Hunts? Similarly, have you ever had Heinz ketchup in Canada? It's sweeter. And yes, you can tell. It's just ketchup. But it matters.

"A brand is a living entity – and it is enriched or undermined cumulatively over time, the product of a thousand small gestures."

Michael Eisner, Former CEO, Disney

A Snake with Fresh Skin

Recognizing you're in need of a Brand Spanking is not a bad thing – it's an opportunity. The decision may be difficult, the process arduous, but the reward is immeasurable. I promise you.

From the smallest logo update or website refresh to the lock, stock and barrel re-brand, this is your opportunity to escape from the dried husk of corporate identity you previously called a "brand" and emerge like a snake with fresh skin – hungry, shiny and ready to strike.

Thirteen Symptoms That Say Your Brand Needs a Spanking

I know it's a difficult decision to make. Unless your business is in total crisis mode, you may be wary of shaking things up. That's why we've put together this short list of symptoms that indicate your brand may be in need of a spanking. If even one of these makes you squirm, you've come to the right place.

1. The Elevator Pitch

Do your employees stutter when asked about your brand? If someone walking by your establishment wonders, "What kind of business is this?" would he stop short after responding with "a shoe store" or "a card shop" or "an electrical supply company"?

At Fitting Group, we decided to test ourselves by taking the "elevator pitch" literally. Starting from the 11th floor of our building, we followed each of our co-workers into the elevator with a video camera and filmed them answering the question, "What is Fitting Group?" They had only the time it took to get to the lobby. And you know what? We rocked it.

Every one of us had more or less the same answer. We all mentioned branding, marketing and creative services. We all mentioned our Challenger Brand focus. Some of us were more confident on camera while others were funnier. Some of us sweat a lot when we're nervous. But in the end, I was proud of our consistency. Trying to view the video through the eyes of a stranger to our agency, I determined that any one of us would have been an adequate brand ambassador – including the interns!

How would you have done? And your employees?

Your lowly interns?

2. You Think Your Product is for Everyone

Here's a hint: no product is one-size-fits-all. No *good* product, that is. (Even the Forever Lazy comes in three models.)

And that's fine, because no business has enough money or bandwidth to try to market to everyone. Which means if you're not clear on who will buy your brand, you're going to waste a lot of resources.

Again, the best way to find out is to ask. When the whole staff, from the person who greets customers at the door or answers your phone, to the CEO and your board of directors, can describe your ideal customer as if he or she was a first cousin, then my friend, you are on your way to branding nirvana.

Of course, most of us in the real world are somewhere else on that scale. The closer you are to the other end, where you are constantly reinventing the way you speak, what you say and who you say it to, based on something other than your strong inner brand compass, the more Spanking you will need.

3. No Competition?

Even companies that provide a product or service that is different from any other on the market have competitors.

A competitor isn't always another brand. It can be "doing it yourself" or even the status quo. A better way to think about this is to ask, "What are the alternatives?" The alternatives could be anything from a different product in the same category, a product from a different category, or no product at all.

No brand is an island.

"You know, at one time there must have been dozens of companies making buggy whips. And I'll bet the last company around was the one that made the best goddamn buggy whip you ever saw."

Danny DeVito in 'Other People's Money'

4. The Meaningless Mission Statement

You may need a Brand Spanking if your mission statement is so generic it should be wrapped in white paper with black letters marked "Brand X."

Get over yourself. This is the time to be humble. Or is it?

When you state your mission, it should authentically reflect the very reason for your company to exist. If it's simply to make as much money as you can, as quickly as you can, perhaps your brand needs more than a Spanking – maybe it needs some prison time. After all, profit without purpose has caused trouble for a lot of people who could benefit from some quiet time behind bars.

Maybe your company hasn't done anything illegal or even unethical; it just hasn't put into words anything truly meaningful about its values and philosophies. When a company tries to please everyone and makes its mission statement so generic that it is literally meaningless, that's criminal, too.

Here are some real life examples from companies you know:

- "...to help people and businesses throughout the world realize their full potential." (Microsoft)
- "...be the best in the eyes of our customers, employees and shareholders." (American Standard)
- "...bringing the best to everyone we touch." – (Estee Lauder)
- "...to connect people to their passions, communities, and the world's knowledge." – (Yahoo!)
- "...providing solutions in real time to meet our customers' needs." – (Halliburton)
- "Guided by relentless focus on our five imperatives, we will constantly strive to implement the critical initiatives required to achieve our vision." – (Albertson's)

Such milquetoast platitudes in a mission statement are generally viewed by employees – and consumers – as hypocrisy. (More on brand authenticity in the second half.)

5. Customer Confusion

You may need a Brand Spanking if in response to "what's their specialty?" your customers never answer consistently. Each and every customer has a totally different view of your company, including the fact that some of them think you sell stuff you don't even sell.

If you asked somebody what the Gatorade brand was about, do you think they'd have the same trouble?

6. Growth and Acquisitions

You may need a Brand Spanking if in the last few years, you've grown tremendously by acquiring other companies and each of those operations still behaves like they always did. Their customers may even still refer to them by their old names.

Changing company culture is always the most difficult thing to do. It requires a great deal of planning and persistent internal brand training. But it's not impossible nor is it futile – just the opposite. It can pay the largest dividends.

7. Sibling Rivalry

You may need a Brand Spanking if there's rivalry between your locations.

Instead of uniting against your competition, your team spends energy and resources trying to best one another. This can happen internally or between multiple offices.

In either instance, it's counter-productive. Your focus remains inward rather than using that energy to collectively wage war on your mutual competitors.

8. Your Leaders "Don't Believe in Branding"

You may need a Brand Spanking if the top marketing officer does not report to the CEO. When this is the case, it is the most blatant signal that the chief executive does not understand or respect branding or marketing. This is disastrous for most companies.

Some common examples include organizations that are run by accountants or engineers. Typically, these folks, smart and well-meaning as they are, have never thought of marketing as anything more than a necessary evil. They know it's not a hard science, but don't appreciate the social science aspect. It's always an afterthought.

Leaders like this may not understand or are unwilling to believe that brand has true equity and that the connection between marketing and the bottom line can increasingly be measured – and measured precisely.

9. The Stiff Breeze

Would your customers cross the street for a seemingly insignificant competitor advantage?

In the retail banking world, the data shows that the threshold for customers' willingness to move their deposit accounts like checking, savings or CDs from one bank to another is about 50 basis points or ½ of 1% more interest as long as there are no penalties for withdrawal.

Forget the math. That means for every thousand dollars in your savings account, you could earn another $5 a year. Five American dollars! That sure doesn't seem like enough to bother about unless you have a boatload of money in the bank or you're angry at your institution for other reasons already – or that the other bank seems attractive for reasons that have nothing to do with the interest rate they are paying.

That's it. The tiniest bit more interest paid on deposits and customers are willing to jump ship. Which means if you win them back with the same strategy, you're just setting yourself up to lose them again to the next stiff breeze. Why not cultivate a more long-lasting perceived difference in your favor?

That difference is your brand.

45

10. The Name Game

You may need a Brand Spanking if even your best customers can't pronounce your name.

People don't like to feel stupid or ignorant and if given a choice, they don't like to feel uncertain. With something as simple as the name of a company or product, why would you want to put a roadblock between you and the customer?

Can you say "L'Occitane?"

11. No One Likes a Despot

Do you and your associates get together behind closed doors and practice your maniacal laughs because your consumers are forced – either through patent or distribution – to buy your product?

That may seem like a golden ticket, but I'd be wary. No one likes monopolies – including our government. Consumers particularly hate to feel as if they are being held hostage by a corporation.

Maybe the choice exists, but it's a costly one. For example, you are the only dry cleaner within two miles or the next most convenient grocery store is much smaller and doesn't have as wide a selection, though their prices are lower. In these examples, that customer may shop at your store but say nasty things about you to others. "They lose my stuff sometimes," or "He jacks up the price because he knows I have to buy it here."

Your customers fervently wish you had some competition because they really don't want to give you their business. And while this all looks good for your bottom line now, remember what happens to despots.

Think how passionately these same patrons will champion an up-and-comer, if only they were given the chance.

47

12. Twinsies

You may need a Brand Spanking if you are constantly being confused with another brand, of a similar name, in the same business.

In some industries it's annoying, like radio stations with very similar call letters. And in some it can be dangerous, like with pharmaceuticals.

In financial services, where it is already difficult to differentiate, why would you want to name your company Ameritrade when eTrade already exists (or vice versa)?

Your consumers have too much going on in their lives to remember whether your company is the good or the bad pizza. Make it easy on them. Differentiate – and they'll reward you.

(Presuming you aren't the bad pizza, of course.)

13. Mistaken Identity

You may need a Brand Spanking if the domain name for your business sounds like something unintended and terrible. Unfortunately, these are real. Though some of these companies must have realized the error of their ways and redirected to more appropriate addresses.

- kidsexchange.net (Kids Exchange)
- penisland.net (Pen Island)
- bitefartcafe.rs (Bitef Art Café)
- whorepresents.com (Who Represents?)
- gotahoe.com (Go Tahoe)

You get the picture.

"Always be a first-rate version of yourself instead of a second-rate version of someone else."

Judy Garland

Brand is Like Love and God

Trying to define brand is a lot like trying to define love or God. We think we know it when we see it. There are lots of ways to list its features and "the expressions of," and certainly it's easier to define what it is *not*.

But in the end, brand, like love or God, is something that, while it has many symbols, boils down to something we *feel*. It makes us act in certain ways and the feelings that drive our actions can be heavily influenced but not directly controlled by the object of our affections or faith. No matter how you try to define them, neither love nor God nor brand can be fully understood until we feel it.

This hasn't stopped many in the business world from trying to equate the features of a brand with its essence.

In the Beginning, There was BRAND

In the beginning, there was BRAND – and brand, in commerce, equaled name and maybe logo and packaging. The world of business was simpler then. There were fewer choices. Every innovation was a complete novelty, like electricity, automobiles, the telephone...or corn flakes. These things seemed miraculous – like heaven on earth. Back then, all you had to do to "brand" was call it by your family name – Bell or Kellogg's or Ford – or by its description – General Electric – because every brand was first to market.

Even then, in the 19th century, brands had their early adopters as well as their detractors. New products mean *change* and some people will always be opposed to change. However, there was a key difference between then and now. Say you saw the telephone as a device poised to erode human communication. How far afield would your voice be heard without the very innovation about which you were skeptical? "Can you hear me now?" used to be answered with awe, not frustration.

Today, people are more educated, less trusting and far less isolated from one another. The world has gotten much more complicated – almost too complicated for the human brain to keep up with it all. The symbols of brand such as name, logo, colors and voice must stand for a lot more nuance – in essence, they become shortcuts.

Collective Experiences

With so much variety and so many choices to be made on a daily basis, brand is more aptly described as the persistent and consistent 'collective' experiences that people have with your product or your company. Therefore, brand is not what makes people discover they need a product.

Instead, brand becomes the reason someone should buy that product from YOU and not someone else.

The Cutco Model

Why do people like Cutco knives so much? To be sure, they are a well-designed and attractive product. But so are Henckel or Wusthof knives. Why buy Cutco then? Especially given their relatively expensive price point and the fact that you can't buy them at places like Macy's. The company doesn't even advertise. (I hate that!)

The Cutco brand is strong because of its primary sales channel.

Cutco recruits college students and newly-minted college graduates who are indoctrinated into the Cutco sales culture and are encouraged to "practice" on their parents, their relatives, their neighbors and friends of their families. These delightful young people enthusiastically pitch people they know, who trust them and want them to succeed. They tout all the superior features of Cutco knives and the benefits of ownership such as lifetime guarantees and free sharpening for the life of the product.

Consumers therefore have a relationship with the Cutco brand that is directly connected to their relationship with the salesperson.

Will you be the one to tell your nephew no? To deny him success in his first job?

This is powerful stuff. It successfully achieves what other brands aim for with millions of dollars of advertising – an emotional connection between brand and consumer that is difficult to break.

Trust Marks

A great brand has a following of people who more or less agree upon the basic values and tenets of the brand, not unlike a religion. To the extent possible, brand owners (the Founder or CEO of the company) like to control and influence those experiences and keep them positive. They'd like to encourage brand enthusiasts (the consumers) to evangelize on behalf of the brand. The very least the brand owners can do is make an exceptional product. But to differentiate the brand from other good products, they must also strive to control the promises they make and the hopes they nurture, so that their customers will get what they expect. Meeting or exceeding customer expectations is an important hallmark of a great brand.

Some say brand symbols have become the new "trust marks" in our society. A trust mark is the symbol of a promise or pledge. One of the most commonly known examples for consumer electronics is the UL symbol for Underwriters Laboratory, a global independent safety science company that certifies that the products that display the symbol meet government or industry standards.

Broadly speaking, the top brands are trust marks for quality and experience. You have certain expectations when you pop the top on a can of Coca-Cola that you wouldn't necessarily have with a lesser-known brand. You have certain expectations when you walk into a McDonald's restaurant that you wouldn't have when you walk into a local Mom & Pop diner.

Brand Communities

Whether you're aware of it or not, there is affinity among and between consumers that trust/use/love certain brands, thus creating communities that take on a life of their own – Nike-wearers, Volkswagen-drivers, Mac-users. This is not unlike meeting a perfect stranger in a church and smiling trustingly because you assume that the two of you have something very important in common – your religion.

"If you want to build a ship, don't drum up people to collect wood and don't assign them tasks and work, but rather teach them to long for the endless immensity of the sea."

Antoine de Saint-Exupery

Seven Traits of Badass Brands

First off, it has nothing to do with the color black.

And it doesn't mean flames on your logo.

It's not a slogan or a mascot or a gimmick.

It's an ethos.

I'm talking about the things that define a brand at its core, the kind of badassery that reverberates out into the world and generates looks, likes and fight-to-the-death brand love. So let's get to it. Here are my Seven Traits of Badass Brands.

1. Says NO to convention

We more often recognize the result of this choice rather than the choice itself — i.e., the '60s VW ads, the Domino Project from Seth Godin, the Radiohead pay-what-you-feel album release and anything else that makes you say, "I've never seen that before…"

2. Can't be easily compared

In 1998, what was Apple *like?*

3. Opinion leaders want to be associated with it

Look what happened when Dan Savage's It Gets Better Project caught the eye of Google Chrome.

4. Has a charismatic CEO

Forget the tired Steve Jobs and Richard Branson references — think: Kiip (pronounced 'keep') CEO Brian Wong or Blake Mycoskie from TOMS Shoes.

5. Makes its customers feel young, hip, smart, unique or positive in some other way

Anyone who wears shoes knows they aren't just for avoiding broken glass. We buy things based on what we think (or what we think we think) defines us as individuals.

6. Employees feel lucky to be working there

Whether it's perks like REI's paid sabbatical or intellectual freedom like Google's 20% Time Program, wooing rabid brand ambassadors is an organic effort.

7. Disrupts the status quo

People remember disruption. For two weeks, we ran a series of billboards the likes of which no one (in Pittsburgh) had ever seen. To this day, when I tell people our company name they say, "Oh, I love seeing your billboards." And we haven't run them since 2006.

It's time to ante up. Is your brand badass?

Penetrating the Everyday

Badass brands cut through the clutter, a task that becomes more difficult with each passing day.

Have you ever considered just how much noise a brand has to cut through to get an iota of attention? The people we want to buy our products and services, no matter who they are or what positions they hold, are focused on their own high priorities.

"What if my daughter doesn't get a job after graduation? Will she want to move back home?" or "Is it going below freezing tonight? Should I cover the flower bed?" or "What's that weird noise the car is making?" or "Does he still love me?"

Any of those things – even the flowers – are probably more important to the average person than your brand. And you can multiply that by five if you're a Challenger Brand.

The reality is we humans have gotten really good at ignoring what is not immediately relevant. Think about how many times you have passed the same street corner with a line of newspaper boxes. Can you name the publications that are in those boxes? What if tomorrow you decided that you wanted to move to a new apartment? Wouldn't it be useful to know that one of those boxes contained *Weekly Apartment Finder*? It didn't matter to you yesterday or the day before, so you never paid attention.

Sloth vs. Survival

Do not mistake these filters for laziness; they are self-preservation. Our brains would explode if we let in every piece of information that passes through one of our senses and tried to remember it.

Do you feel the sock on your heel? What about your tongue on the roof of your mouth?

Sure, you do now, but I'll bet you didn't notice either of them just 30 seconds ago.

This self-preservation mechanism is even better-developed in our work lives. When people have their business hats on, they are more adept at filtering things out. That could be because they're more concerned with their daily productivity, or they are so overloaded with work that they shut out any new information that is not critical. Another reason could be that they actively shun considering new information or making any changes because change might result in greater workload.

Now That I've Got You Here

So let's say you get past this first, great hurdle – you've gotten someone's attention. There are a number of other layers that have to be penetrated before someone actually buys your product. If we're lucky, these layers are penetrated in rapid succession, and a buying decision can seem almost instantaneous. Or, if our products require more thought, analysis or consideration, the buying cycle might take a long time or worse, never be completed at all.

The factors that influence how long a decision takes and the steps we have to go through are closely related to the dollar value of the purchase and the perceived risk of buying your brand.

The higher the price, the more resistant the buyer.

You almost never buy the first car you test drive. The last time you bought a car, how many dealerships did you visit? How much research did you do online? How many people did you talk to?

What about the last house you purchased? Because the risk of making the wrong decision is so high, you need almost an overload of information, features, and third-party endorsements about the neighborhood, the school district, the resale value, inspections and lots and lots of haggling over the price. Guarantees and added value, like the seller leaving the refrigerator or the washer and dryer to sweeten the deal, will positively influence the outcome.

The higher the price, the more resistant the buyer. But the price is not always in dollars and cents.

The Southwest State of Mind

"If in the event you couldn't control yourself and just HAD to bring that big honkin' carryon aboard – even though we don't charge anything for checked baggage – we will be forced to throw your belongings onto the tarmac and leave them behind, but not before we rifle through for the presence of chocolate."

That's the Southwest flight attendant telling us they were out of overhead storage. Everybody laughed. No one was offended. And now I'm putting it in this book. Could she have made an impatient, scolding announcement? Sure. But this was Southwest Airlines – and people have a certain expectation of this brand.

What makes the Southwest brand so strong? I assure you, it has little to do with the design or colors of their logo. Southwest has a strong brand because people agree the airline treats them fairly, offers competitive pricing and provides an enjoyable experience. People agree that Southwest Airline's staff members seem to love their jobs and have fun doing them, including customers in on the jokes and thereby making travel a little less hectic and irksome.

If you've ever flown on Southwest, you know that instead of having assigned seat numbers and paying extra for first class or an inch more of legroom, seating is first-come, first-served. On a recent Southwest flight, toward the end of the boarding process, the flight attendant announced, "The next empty seat you see is yours. Don't pass it up!"

Their gate areas are more comfortable than usual. They have cushy chairs, computer bars and electrical outlets for your laptop. Many even have small tables and chairs for kids.

All of this contributes to the perceived value of Southwest. Brand entails much more than just creating symbols – the logo, the name, the tagline, the value proposition, etc. Good brands cultivate a collective of positive experiences that a group of people agree embodies a company – an experience people talk about with similar, consistent language.

An experience people will line up to purchase.

Branding Begets Branding

Everyone has experienced over-hype. Overzealous endorsement can often trigger the opposite effect. The more you hear such-and-such movie is the greatest cinematic experience of all time, the less likely you are to feel that way.

Guess what. The same thing happens with brands. The iCult has given birth to a whole demographic of people who care less about features than being just another mindless rider on the bandwagon. (Ironically, this was the exact strategy Apple employed against Microsoft in the now-famous "1984" Super Bowl ad.)

The point is, it's not enough to claim to be fun. In its quest to challenge all the other airlines, Southwest actually had to **BE** fun. And that meant ingraining fun into their business, from their employees' demeanor down to their baggage fees and seating policy. In other words, they had to act.

That action is what takes guts. Thinking is a necessary precursor to action. But action is required to achieve success. You can't just think your way to positive outcomes, despite the title of a famous book, *Think and Grow Rich*.

For its original approach to air travel, Southwest has been rewarded with a conspiratorial media. Because the company has become known for its humor and traveler-friendly attitude, the media likes to cover people's experiences, thereby providing those who have never flown with the company a vicarious positive experience.

More importantly, it tempts people who are not already customers to experience it for themselves.

Luck is Just Hard Work Re-Branded

For many years all kinds of very smart people have been studying, writing and offering theories about the best way to do business. Rows and rows of books line the shelves in libraries and bookstores, not to mention gigabytes of digital data, touting every possible approach to branding, marketing, advertising, public relations, and now social media. Because there are no 'natural laws' of business like there are in science, most of this bottomless pool of information is not much more than opinion – sometimes informed and experienced opinion – but opinion nonetheless.

We all want to believe there is a simple solution to our problems – some magic potion, silver bullet, or wave of the wand that will grant every wish without the accompanying hard work.

But in our hearts, we already know where to look. First, you need to have a solid product or service that improves the lives of our customers.

Then all you have to do is work like the dickens.

The Dickens is in the Details

The phrase "like the dickens" has nothing to do with the English writer, Charles. Like "what the deuce," dickens was a stand-in curse for "the devil." So when Shakespeare used it in *The Merry Wives of Windsor*, his audience would have understood it to be a polite way to call on the devil.

Since I told you that branding was like god and love somewhere back there, you'll understand that the devil has his role to play in the details. So now that you've accepted the fact that you will have to work hard, it's time to talk about the particulars.

To maximize the effect of your efforts, I recommend focusing on four ingredients.

1. Awareness

And there are two ways you can go about this.
1. Money
2. Intelligence

Awareness does not have scruples. If you have enough money, you can buy it six ways to Sunday. Advertising will do the trick – the more advertising, the better. The better the advertising, meaning the simpler and more compelling the message, the more people will try your product. If your product is a good and useful one and your customer has a positive first experience, you are more likely to get to step two, Preference. This part is fairly formulaic and well-tested, if not an immutable law.

But what if your advertising budget pales in comparison to your competitors'? Trying to outspend or even keep up with the race could then be a very costly and potentially ruinous course.

Lucky for you, Awareness can also be courted. It is has a weak spot for ingenuity, creativity and risks. Viral, guerilla, grassroots and social media campaigns are now touted as David's sling.

Just one problem. Have you ever used a slingshot to slay a murderous giant? Yeah, I didn't think so. Before you go and get his attention, it might be best to take your budget, however meager, and hire some professionals. This will also save you from poking your own eye out.

2. Preference

Presuming you've succeeded in making a customer aware of your brand, now you must make her prefer it over another. When confronted with a choice, she needs a reason to choose you more often than the other guy. Especially the first time!

This reason could be any of a thousand value propositions. The easiest factor – and most volatile – is price. You can be the low cost choice, but only until another brand resets pricing below yours. Reacting creates a downward spiral that may benefit the customer, but is disastrous for your business. Eventually, every sale will cost you money instead of making you some. Clearly, this is not a sustainable model and is usually more damaging to a brand than not. Contrary to a statement I once heard from some knucklehead, you can't "lose money on every sale but make it up on volume."

Instead, let's talk about a better way to create preference. You can start by adding value that is appreciated by the customer beyond what it costs you to provide it.

For example, at my hair salon, the young lady that washes hair for the stylist before the cut and sweeps the hair off the floor during and after, also gives hand massages while you sit in the stylist's chair getting your hair cut. That employee is already being paid a wage, therefore the extra service doesn't cost any more than the price of the dab of hand cream she uses. But the payoff for the customer is big.

I love the attention and the extra service. It makes me feel good physically, less bored mentally and, as a bonus, I'm inclined to tip the young lady who provided the service. That gives her an incentive do a good job and a reason to appreciate the opportunity her employer gave her to make a few extra bucks. If she's really a go-getter, she may even recommend the hand cream, which of course, they sell in their shop.

3. Loyalty

Gaining customers' awareness and preference will mean nothing in the long run if you can't keep them. Loyalty, like courage and character, is best demonstrated when your customer is challenged.

Back to my hair salon example – I have been a loyal customer for over fifteen years. And in that time, I've learned of newer salons, perhaps ones that were closer to my home or offering special prices. Still, I go to *my* salon – but why?

Well, my stylist is very good. That helps. When I first started going to her, the price was right in line with all the other options I had near that location. Over the years, she has regularly raised her prices, so now I pay a pretty steep price for my hair cuts, even though I consider my needs to be fairly modest – I don't need any special treatments and I'm not at all fussy.

But even though I'm aware that I'm paying too much, I am still loyal because they keep upping the ante on the service. Over the years they have added automated appointment reminders, scalp massages, the aforementioned hand massage, coffee, water, wine and herbal tea choices brought to me "chair-side," high-quality robes and a smattering of other pampering touches and incentives to remain a customer. It would be very difficult for me to make a change now.

81

At every turn, I am reminded by their behavior that they value my business. So I stay.

4. Evangelism

Brand evangelism is the holy grail and the seventh plane. It's realizing you're levitating during meditation, reincarnation as a fire breathing dragon and dark coffee after a big meal. Many of you have never reached this mountaintop – but striving for it should be a factor in every decision you make.

There are many reasons for a customer to choose your product. Many more for them to continue to buy it. But for consumers to become evangelists, it requires a special relationship between the brand and the person. Think about the people who will only drive a Honda, the ones who drink nothing but Yuengling Beer. These people no longer choose what vehicle or beverage to purchase. Their selection is locked in, automatic. They can feel it in their gut.

And on top of all the other great features they enjoy about their brand, these steadfast few enjoy a final benefit – the luxury of already knowing what works. Life has become so wrought with choices, sometimes it's comforting to know that no matter what else happens, at least you can count on [wouldn't you like to insert your brand name here?].

Evangelism is the most powerful weapon in the Challenger Brand's arsenal. To wield it, you must set whatever brought you to this business aside – money, family, fame.

I don't care if you sell dryer sheets or divorce counseling. From now on, your mission is to cultivate a brand that makes your customer's life better.

This is how brands earn evangelists. And it's how Challenger Brands grapple to the top of the pile.

Fluff and Serve

In short, the Challenger Brand's strategic plan should include a path that moves customers through the cycle of discovery (awareness), repeat purchase (preference), steadfastness in the face of competing offers (loyalty) and persuading others to buy, too (evangelism).

"I have found no greater satisfaction than achieving success through honest dealing and strict adherence to the view that, for you to gain, those you deal with should gain as well."

Alan Greenspan

Brand Persona

Everyone knows that actions speak louder than words. But rarely do business people comprehend that this tenet applies just as much to brands. In fact, many of the principles, practices and precepts conceived and written about human behavior also apply to brands – some good, some not so much.

- Like ordinary people, ordinary brands also seek the safety of numbers.
- Like smart people, smart brands can quickly learn lessons from observation rather than trial and error.
- For both people and brands, it's important to be beautiful on the inside.

This is often surprisingly hard to appreciate, until you stop to think about the phrase 'brand persona.' What is a brand persona if not the anthropo-morphizing of a commercial or not-for-profit entity? With young companies, you sometimes need to do no more to understand the brand persona than to meet the founder. With long established companies where the founder is gone, the clues are a little more elusive.

I find the concept of brand persona very useful. Advertising creative departments all over the world do, too. One of the standard practices in brand development is to ask the question, "If your brand was a person, how would you describe him... Or is it her?"

Challenger Brand Modus Operandi

Challenger Brands think up forceful, sometimes crazy (meaning unrealistic from the point of view of most people) strategies for growth. They sniff out opportunities for exposure like a hungry grizzly clawing up clams. To do this, you must:

- Behave differently than your competitors
- Take specific, clearly defined actions and communicate in highly differentiating words
- Draw attention by being fun to talk about – i.e., be provocative
- Stand out not so much because of your words, but because of what you are willing to do
- Fear not the consequences

If you're a Challenger, what's at stake is not what you stand to lose, but what you stand to win. Challengers are willing to sacrifice far beyond the point where average folk would throw in the towel. They view risk not framed in terms of scarcity but in terms of the abundance that will be the prize.

Talk is cheap. It's *behavior* that has a price. And perseverance is the most costly and risky behavior of all.

But it is perseverance in the face of obstacles that pays large rewards. That's why we call them Challenger Brands.

Value of Branding

Branding plays a fundamental role in attracting customers to your business. It also plays a role in telling you who makes a good customer and who doesn't.

For example, I know I'm facing a mismatch when I'm talking to an entrepreneur or a CEO who says, "We can't afford to spend any money on branding. We just need to concentrate on things that will lead directly to a sale."

At this point in the conversation I look for a convenient and gracious way to pick up my marbles and go home. After nearly a quarter of a century in business, I've done my time trying to convince the hardheaded number-cruncher or the professional skeptic who will just never, ever believe in the power of branding.

C'est la freaking vie.

As an agency with a clear mission to Challengers, I finally know it's not my job to convince this person that branding is worth his investment. It's my job to connect with customers who already know this – and who are ready to take the gutsy path to glory.

The Pervasiveness of Brands

"I am immune to branding and advertising. It absolutely doesn't work on me."

A guy named Al says this to me. He is logical and rational and he believes it when he says it. I love meeting guys like Al.

"Really?" I say. "What kind of car do you drive?"

Al is a self-made, successful businessman who was the first in his family to go to college. He is proud of the fact that his wife "doesn't have to work" and stays at home raising their kids. He's wearing a crisp white shirt with his monogram embroidered on the cuffs and a little too much expensive aftershave. I predict Al drives a car that reflects how he sees himself and how he wants others to see him. In other words, I predict that Al drives a car that is branded to create an impression of success.

When buying his vehicle, Al probably had a list of two or three cars that interested him. He forgot, or maybe never gave a conscious thought to, their marketing messages, their price point and the impressions he had about who else drove those kinds of cars. He may have asked a few friends or family members. He may be trying to emulate someone he admires. And he may have test driven all of them...or not.

So when Al replied, "I simply decided one day that I was only going to drive Jaguars from now on," I had to stifle a laugh. He gave no rationale or logical reason for his long-term commitment to the Jaguar brand. Nor did he realize that his decision was based solely on his perception of the brand – a perception so powerful, that it overwhelmed any second thoughts he may have had since the Jaguar brand has been batted about for the last few years between parent companies. I wonder if Al knows the chairman of the company that builds his Jaguar is actually Ratan Tata – since the brand is now owned by Tata Motors, a huge Indian conglomerate.

But he's "immune to branding." Sure.

Unbank

Because I know and have invested in my own brand, I know to quickly identify the Al's of the world and move on. My mission is to serve people like you, the reader who understands that brands are incredibly powerful. Generally speaking, people like Al don't seek out the services of my agency. Our brand sorts it out before we even get to the conversation about cars. Both sides are better off with this arrangement. In other words, the brand is doing its job.

Branding doesn't guarantee smooth sailing with all customers who align with your brand, but it keeps you moving in the right track – most likely the winning track over the long haul.

For example, think about the new age of banking. In an industry like financial services, products are not usually created to benefit customers as much as they benefit the bottom line of the bank. And the advertising style of banks, given that they are usually very conservative and even buttoned-down, is typically predictable, bordering on dull. Certainly, that makes banks risk adverse – not usually a good fit for Challenger Brand thinking.

Big banks are busy trying to compete for what's left of the best customers and salvage what they can from the mortgage meltdown while placating the regulators. Smaller banks are trying to survive and the ones that are managing to do so are hunkering down until the sun comes out again. And like any major disruption in business, there are opportunities for the fearless and visionary.

So it's not that surprising that I found myself and my philosophy in the right place at the right time in the banking industry – but it wasn't easy or painless to get there.

Sometimes Challenger Brand thinking means our ideas are ahead of their time.

So here's how one conversation went in the year 2007. Seeing the regulatory environment loosen up and allow more competition, plus the trend in online banking, here's what I said to a banking client.

Me: "We think you should change the name of your bank to Unbank. We'll advertise that you're a new kind of bank – completely transparent, with no hidden fees or evil practices. Unbank takes the pain out of the banking relationship for the customer. You'll launch new products with no minimum balance requirements, no penalties for early withdrawal or loan payoffs, no ATM fees, etc."

Client: "What? But how will we make money? We can't do that!"

Me: "You'll make money the traditional way, a tiny bit from each customer. Plus you'll add some new services. And you'll do it all online, so you'll dramatically increase the number of customers you have without adding any significant overhead by building branches. You don't even have to increase your advertising budget by much at first. You'll be putting your ads online, a much more cost effective way to get the word out."

Client: "We'll give it some thought."

Me: (six months later) "Have you thought about it?"

Client: "We're still thinking about it."

Me: (six more months later) "Have you thought about it?"

Client: "We're still trying to figure it out."

Banking crisis happens.

Me: (six more long months later) "Time is running out. Someone else will do it first."

Client: "We've decided it's not such a great idea. We'll just hunker down until things get better."

And then we see a commercial on TV for Ally Bank.

Hard Pill to Swallow

In hindsight, it is easy to see why this client would hesitate to take our advice. As much as they want to believe our Challenger Brand philosophy and beat the competition, there are never any guarantees of success when you are blazing new trails. No way to measure anticipated ROI. No way to avoid other people's mistakes. No way to review what others have done, because they haven't yet.

We totally understand the client's point of view: it's troublesome to think you might not succeed – especially if you have shareholders to answer to. Sometimes the barrier to doing provocative things is fear of being laughed at or ridiculed.

Well, actually, that's a given. Competitors will mock you... until you succeed. Then they'll stop laughing. We know this because we lived it.

"First they ignore you, then they
laugh at you, then they fight you,
then you win."

Mahatma Gandhi

Walk the Walk

There are reasons for clichés such as "no guts, no glory" or "nothing ventured, nothing gained." We don't make our recommendations lightly or without serious thought to the business consequences for the client. And we walk the walk.

So it was that we were left with our ideas but no client who would take advantage of them… until now. Along comes a Challenger like Unbank – ok, that's not their real name, but it's too early to disclose that! – rising up like a phoenix out of the financial debacle dust.

They have brave new ideas and the guts to try them. We have the industry know-how, both on the financial services side and the branding side. It might be a marriage made in heaven; only time will tell. But we never would have even gotten invited to the party if we hadn't already established an unassailable brand ourselves as Challenger Brand champions. In addition, we had been thinking about the opportunities and watching the horizon for just such a fledging organization with a voracious appetite to grow.

This is how it works. Know your brand. Stick with it. Practice. Be ready. Act.

Attack.

Sweat Equity

Brands have value far beyond the total tangible assets of a company and are often the most important, if not always conscious, decision-making tools. Branding creates clarity and consistency throughout the organization, leading customers to have an experience that meets with their expectations.

Of course, that kind of value isn't free. Building brands – especially brands worth their snuff – costs money. A company must invest resources to build it, just as it invests in a website, an advertising campaign or any other business-generating asset.

The difference is, with branding, a great deal of that investment will be in sweat equity rather than dollars. Branding requires daily monitoring throughout all levels of a company to ensure that the brand is being supported and expressed in a consistent and clearly communicated way. Even minor missteps can undo the work of your massive investments. Worse – or at least more complicated – the CEO and leadership aren't the only ones who can affect this outcome.

Trickle Up Branding

Branding starts at the top with the founder or the CEO, but every employee and representative of an organization has a vital role to play in branding. If you doubt this for even a moment, think about a large corporation you dislike and ask yourself what caused you to feel this way?

Was it a conversation with the President in which she admitted commitment to shareholder value at the expense of doing what is right for the environment? Not likely.

Was it something you read in the newspaper about a heinous crime perpetrated on unsuspecting consumers by the corporate executives? It's possible.

Or was it simply that the last time you interacted with the company's sales or service people they behaved insensitively toward you or refused to give you satisfaction? Ding, ding, ding – I'm looking at you, Comcast.

Now consider that in your estimation, the brand of that enormous company was perhaps forever tarnished by someone who may have been nothing more than an hourly employee having a bad day. (This might not be Comcast's only shortcoming, but you get my drift.)

The Brand & The Product

A question that I'm sometimes asked is whether it makes more sense to focus on building the brand of the corporate entity itself or on the company's products. This is an artificial question because the corporate reputation and the popularity and success of its products go hand-in-hand. Giant corporate brands can be undone by mediocre or out-of-touch or failing products. Think: Toyota and brake pedals.

Service company brands are largely dependent on meeting the quality expectations of their customers. Some people are willing to pay a much higher price for a stay at a Fairmont hotel rather than a Sheraton because they believe the brand promise, even if they've never experienced the particular property at their destination. People have been promised, and expect to enjoy, a very high level of service in a luxury environment at a Fairmont hotel. But if Fairmont should begin to use lower quality products, let their properties get run down, or fail to nurture the company culture or properly train and hold their employees to a high standard of excellence, it won't be long before guests notice and complain or worse, simply stop checking in to Fairmont hotels. When experiences are not aligned with promise, the brand suffers. When the expectations don't reach or aren't enforced at every level of the organization, especially at every contact with the customer, the brand suffers. And in the hyper-connected world of social media, it happens in

101

the time it takes to type 140 characters and hit "tweet."

There is little mystery about the relationship between brand perceptions and sales. Granted, it is usually impossible to trace the precise relationship between a given "random act of branding" and a sale. But the more people say favorable things about a company, the better the bottom line results. In contrast, it doesn't take too many negative reviews or comments to drive people away from any association with a tainted brand.

Branding requires careful nurturing over time. It requires communicating the same messages over and over and over again. It requires controlling the "voice" of the company throughout all communications to the extent possible. In writing, this is relatively easy.

When you have a large workforce and many people who have contact with customers, it is more difficult and requires more effort on the part of, what should be, a brand management team. The brand management team should include the CEO, CMO, marketing department and Sales Manager. The main thing to understand is that *everyone* has a role to play in brand building.

The New Normal

Is branding as fundamental today as it was in the past? Some say we are living in a time of a "New Normal" and that business has changed in a profound way from the beginning of the first decade of the 21st century to the end of that decade.

If so, then what are the implications for the concept of BRAND – is it more or less important than it was? Should we put more thought into proactively creating and managing the brand experience? Should we devote more resources in shaping and defending the brand? And if the answer is yes to one or more of these questions, then by what means can we achieve this control and what can we expect as a return on our investment?

To be sure, these are important questions for marketers of all stripes – from agency denizens to company product managers. But none are so affected as entrepreneurs and Firebrands. (More on Firebrands in Book 2… I promise.)

Everybody has an Opinion

In the new normal, the world is perceived as a dangerous place made all the more suspect by big business involvement. Just try to think about BP without calling to mind the Gulf oil spill. (Or GE and the near meltdown of its nuclear power plants in Japan.) If it wasn't before, big business is now on the radar of the common man.

Now more than ever, conversations between families, friends and colleagues at the dinner table and water cooler are about how tough times are, who's to blame and what "they" are doing about it. People want to feel smart and in-the-know. So people tell others about their opinions, describing the brands they love; the value, quality, consistency and dependability of the brands they use; the places they shop; and the honesty and integrity of the people they have come to trust.

The clearer, more unique and more interesting your brand messages are, the more your core customers and evangelists can not only repeat them back to you, but can convincingly share them with others.

Reinforce those messages now and you will win new loyal customers. Think of your branding and marketing efforts as the lubricant that makes peer-to-peer endorsements easier to communicate. Take advantage of the power of social networking, social media, and social bookmarking.

Coming Clean

As important as brand management is though, at the end of the day, it's still a means to an end. Simply put, we manage our brand because we want to sell more stuff at the highest possible price. (You didn't think we were branding for branding's sake, did you?) To do this, we need to earn the trust of the consumer.

Trust is a critical value point – and it's the primary currency of brand-building. Brand logos have become trust-marks in our society and have created affinity groups among and between consumers. Logos have practically taken on a life of their own.

I am convinced that the key to brand owners maintaining a large degree of control in the time of the New Normal is to view every sale as being accompanied by that trust-mark – that promise to the customer that says, "You'll get your money's worth and our product will perform as expected."

Why? Because the logo says so.

"The glue that holds all
relationships together –
including the relationship
between the leader and the led –
is trust, and trust is based on
integrity."

Brian Tracy

Strategies & Tactics ≠ Branding

Strategic plans and tactics change over time and are subject to external forces such as economic conditions, new technologies, consumer tastes and the competitive landscape.

Branding is much more fundamental and immutable than strategic plans. Brand building is a long-term process, not an event. Remember our definition of Brand – the collective experience had by the consumer that we must nurture and guide. It involves all stages of business administration, from vision to planning to execution to garnering feedback to measuring results.

The Brand must be stable, solid and reliable. It must be based on a point-of-view, a philosophy. It should be guided by a set of clearly understood and articulated values. The purpose of branding is to nurture and foster preference and loyalty among people who can most use, or best appreciate, the company's products and services.

Guidestars

At the moment your brand begins to come into clear focus, you ought to start to formulate guidelines for behavior. In business, this is something we have to do deliberately and consciously. The beginning of brand development is the period when an organization is actively figuring out what it wants to stand for and how it can demonstrate this intent. Once the groundwork is laid, there isn't much room for missteps in business – people quickly begin to have a clear expectation of how a brand should behave. When that expectation is not met, people vote with their wallets and with negative talk. I often make analogies between business brands and individuals. In creating a brand guidestar, there are significant differences.

In life, the period for developing a guidance system is long and often subconscious. Most people just obey their parents and teachers, follow their noses and arrive at adulthood never giving much thought to where their playbook came from. People have their entire childhoods to develop this process of formulating personal guidelines. Childhood is for testing limits and rules and the boundaries of every aspect of your world, the physical, the empirical and the theoretical. We mostly do this unconsciously and one day at a time. I'm sure if you thought about it, you could name a few significant incidents in your life that helped shape who you are. As for me, I remember certain things people said to me as my personality was developing that helped me become who I am.

"You're very direct. I like that about you," or "I like that you say exactly what you mean. I never have to guess what you're thinking." Because I felt this was a desirable trait, I then went out of my way to embrace it.

Brands also evolve over their lifetimes, but a brand has the advantage of not needing to reach maturity to figure it out. The presumably mature executive decision-makers that shape the personality of the brand also are responsible for creating the guidelines for its behavior so that everyone who represents the brand can internalize, understand and behave consistently with brand guidelines.

Sugar and Spice and Everything Nice

What do brand guidelines consist of? The visual brand identity – things like logo, typeface, colors – are just the tip of the iceberg, the part that you can see. They are highly symbolic of what's "underneath." Alas, many brand owners never go any further in thinking about their brands than these symbols.

Some companies spend years and tens of thousands of dollars designing these things. They end up with aesthetically sophisticated logos, inviting color schemes and beautifully laid out stationery, signage and advertising. They create elaborate graphic design and brand standards manuals, compelling everyone in the company to adhere to these inviolable laws. Heaven forbid a color is off a few shades or a logo gets stretched out of proportion. These heinous acts might jeopardize the future of the company.

While these disrespectful brand acts might indicate a lack of know-how or the tools needed to ensure consistency with such things, I don't believe that they are the root cause of brand ruin, unless there is no respect for the real essence of the brand in the first place. Everything a company does, absolutely everything, should be determined by the credo of the brand. This is how brand integrity is maintained. But let's start with the visual and the voice.

The Clothes & the Brand

It has been said many times and in many ways that "clothes do not make the man." But you could argue clothes shape the way the man behaves in any given situation.

When it comes to brands, the visual cues set the tone for how people will perceive the brand in the absence of any additional information or before they have had a first-hand experience. If you doubt this, think about the last time you were in a shoe store that displayed the stacked boxes of shoes. Did you make any snap judgments about the shoes? Did you favor one pair over another based partially on the packaging?

For Challenger Brands, the symbols that make up the brand identity can be even more important than usual. They can make the difference between a door in the face or a foot in the door.

Andrea F. Fitting

Five Rules of Challengers

1. Be rebellious.
2. Be un-ignorable.
3. Be clear about your values.
4. Be a dreamer.
5. Be on the interwebs*.

(*not a new thing...just slang...see urban dictionary)

What Would Brandee Do?

When we created Brandee as the iconic symbol of Brand Spanking and the Fitting Group agency, we could hardly wipe the smiles from our faces. We felt, deep in our guts, that we had epitomized the second Challenger Brand rule – be un-ignorable. Next we had to define the guidelines for *Brandee Behavior*.

We started asking "What would Brandee do?" when we had any sort of business decision to make. For example, in the hiring process, not only did we think about whether a candidate would fit in, but we developed our interview questions in such a way as to ferret out a more predictive picture of how well that candidate would represent our brand.

In other words, was the candidate an advocate for Challenger Brand thinking? Was he or she able to speak authoritatively about the subject he or she claimed to have expertise in? Was he an active listener? Was she energetic? Did he or she have a well-developed sense of humor?

Could they wrap their minds in leather and crack a bullwhip?

The Meek & Mediocre Need Not Apply

Through Brandee's eyes, we are able to see more clearly that people who have taken calculated risks and have shown fearlessness in the face of obstacles in their own lives are more likely to be credible advisors and consultants to the clients of our agency as we suggest to them to do the same. Turnabout is fair play.

Just as a brand for which style and panache are important brand equities would be better served by representatives who are outwardly stylish and exude charisma, Fitting Group gains credibility from representatives who are confident, direct and always remind clients about the strategic underpinnings of the creative and tactical course they are on, even when the clients begin to have second thoughts. Being a Challenger Brand is not for the meek. So having meek team members at Fitting Group just doesn't usually work out very well. This is how our hiring guidelines came to be.

This is how Brandee's perspective became our guidestar. Having a symbol through which to express your brand persona makes it a little easier to test your plans for brand consistency. And everything should be tested, from your HR policies to your client appreciation gestures to the layout of your facilities. The more you follow your guidestar, the clearer and more differentiated your brand will become to your internal audience as well as your customers and would-be customers.

Any time we get caught up on a pivotal decision, the path to an answer is as simple as asking WWBD?

"Be who you are and say what you feel because those who mind don't matter and those who matter don't mind."

Dr. Seuss

Authenticity

Of all of the content in this book and all of my beliefs about business in general and Challenger Brands specifically, being authentic is the most universally understood and embraced. Why then are there so many companies that none of us would characterize as being authentic? This is yet another important opportunity for Challengers.

Market leaders, especially the very large ones, have a lot of things to worry about, not the least of which are quarterly financial performance and remaining at the top of the heap. Many of these companies, once Challengers themselves, have become victims of their own success in two crucial ways.

Goliath Syndrome

Deliberately or inadvertently, many Goliaths mistakenly make market leadership the core of their brand. They may have forgotten their more humble roots or just stopped talking about them. Now they focus on closing the gates behind them so others have to struggle to keep up.

This means that a good amount of energy has to be dedicated to making the cash register ring, and in some cases, though admittedly not all, that is done at the expense of authenticity.

We Love an Underdog

The second misstep made by many market leaders is one of positioning.

From Rocky and Rudy to the Brave Little Toaster, popular culture is riddled with the tales of underdogs. The American Revolution, the 300 Spartans at Thermopylae and, of course, David and Goliath – these stories, rote as they may be, hold a powerful place in our subconscious.

The less likely a protagonist is to win, the more we hope she will.

Whether they know it or not, brands do themselves a disservice by playing the uncontested champion. We are given to automatically root for the up-and-comers, even if we don't know much about either option. What's more, consumers who align with underdog brands get a sense of individuality by doing so – even if everybody else is doing the exact same thing, as is the case with the iPhone. Rooting for an underdog makes you feel like part of a movement and connects you to the kind of aspirational thinking embodied by all Challengers.

Think about America's antitrust and monopoly laws. Salary caps in professional sports. Bans on performance-enhancing drugs in the Olympics.

119

Andrea F. Fitting

There's something in us constantly striving for equality, a leveling of the playing field. Market leaders aren't inherently evil. They have many admirable qualities. Is it Goliath's fault he was born large, strong and skilled at swordplay? No, but we'd much rather hold up David for his bravery and cleverness.

Psychology shows that we are powerfully motivated to be fair. We are naturally attracted to companies we perceive to be fairer, companies that work harder to win or keep our loyalty – think about the legendary "We Try Harder" campaign from Avis. We're especially fond of companies that appear to be at some disadvantage as a result of unfair practices by the market leader. They need our help to succeed, and we support them time and time again.

The Challenger Compass

Because of these reasons, Challengers on their way up find it easier to differentiate because they are getting a psychological boost from us. What will become vitally important for them is to remain authentic and retain their start-up stories as part of their brand no matter how much they succeed. Challenger Brands will be able to more easily attract the right kind of customer, the kind who really wants its product or service, and would be willing to pay a premium for it.

A good brand, like an upstanding citizen, has a moral compass that guides its behavior and predicts its conduct. The authenticity of a brand is reinforced each time a customer has a positive encounter with the brand – real or virtual. Because the brand has integrity and is consistent, the kind of customer who most enjoys that brand and keeps coming back to purchase more from the company is consistent, too. And this self-fulfilling cycle becomes key to helping Challenger Brands express their authenticity in their marketing and advertising.

Andrea F. Fitting

The 3 W's (& an H)

Being consistent and authentic with current and past customers is one thing. We do that through our business practices and processes, the quality of our products and maintaining the level of our service. But how do we communicate our brand authenticity with would-be customers – those who have never had a real experience with us and have yet to purchase what we're selling? Here comes the vital role of marketing and advertising in brand development.

The sole purpose of marketing is to set the stage for sales.

- Who – marketing must identify the likely buyer
- Where – marketing must anticipate where that buyer will be
- What – marketing must determine how to communicate what to say
- How – marketing must figure out the best and most cost efficient way to get that message across.

Authenticity and an honest evaluation or analysis of a Challenger Brand's best customers leads to the ability of the brand to plan out its marketing strategies and tactics to the utmost efficiency and benefit for attracting new ones.

122

Don't Outspend, Outwit

In almost all cases, Challengers have less money and fewer resources of any kind than the market leaders. This would seem like a very discouraging problem if all else were equal. But fortunately, things are not equal and as I've described, Challenger Brands have behavioral psychology on their side.

Once Fitting Group determined that its brand was going to revolve around the notion of rule-breaking and evocative irreverence, it was natural to conclude that people who wanted to build Challenger organizations would be the most likely, most receptive audience for our brand of marketing strategy and advice. We knew that the market leaders had too much at stake or were too cautious to break industry rules. After all, they were the ones who made those rules in the first place.

We didn't want to be disingenuous. We also knew that we didn't want the smaller but timid or ultra conservative company leaders either. We weren't interested in those who were measuring their success in tenths of percentage points in sales.

And the last thing we wanted was to waste our time on those who demanded ads that were saying exactly what every other competitor was saying, brands who subscribed to the theory that there is safety in numbers.

Challengers aren't wildebeests, after all. We are leopards.

"Because It's Cool"

Years ago, before 'The Cloud' meant anything more than the white fluffy thing in the sky, I had a meeting with a company president who lacked insight into the relationship a company must have with its customers to succeed.

The president in question – let's call him Davis – was presiding over a three-year-old company. His product was a data storage device. So far, the venture had been funded by friends and family. Davis was a technician who engineered a product because he could, not because anyone ever said she needed or wanted such a thing. He didn't tell me that in so many words. Instead, Davis rattled off a lot of jargon, most of which I did not understand, until I finally just had to ask, "Have you ever sold a unit?"

Davis answered, "Not yet, but I have a beta-customer who is testing it for free."

"Okay, so who will buy your product?"

Davis thought any business that had to store a lot of data securely should buy his product. I asked him who the market leader was that he would compete against. He named a really large, successful, well-known brand. I asked if Davis' product would sell for a significantly lower price than the leading product in that category.

125

"No, just the opposite. My product costs three times as much – but it has ten times the capacity and is five times more secure than any product on the market."

I countered, "Will customers care about that, even if they have to pay three times more? Will they be able to recoup their investment?"

"Not exactly," Davis said, shifting uncomfortably in his chair. "It's kind of like insurance. Their data will be safer, so they can add 'more reliability' as a selling point." He actually put air quotes around 'more reliability' when he said this.

Before I spend my time meeting with potential clients I always ask a vital question: In a perfect world, who is your ideal customer and why should he buy? The answer will determine whether I take the next step or politely get off the phone as soon as possible.

Davis is a somewhat laughable example, but unfortunately, he's not alone out there. You would be astonished at the number of times I've heard answers to the first part of the question like, "I'm not exactly sure." "People who eat in restaurants." "Women." "Anyone in the English-speaking world, until we have it translated. Then, everyone."

The answer to the 'why should they buy' part of the question is usually something like, "Because it's cool."

At which point, it's time to hang up.

"This may seem simple, but you need to give customers what they want, not what you think they want. And, if you do this, people will keep coming back."

John Ilhan

The Customers

In a perfect world, you could define *customer* with fabulous specificity – that ideal person to conjure up when you are planning your marketing strategy and tactics. This "Mr. or Ms. Right" is the star of your marketing show – the reason your company exists and certainly the reason you have created your products and services.

You, the selfless lover, want to make your customers happy. You want to make their lives easier, healthier, more entertaining, more convenient, or more something that they will appreciate and be happy to pay for. Or you want to empower your target customers with the ability to do something they couldn't do before.

In some cases you are the star of your own marketing show. In other words, sometimes you are the prototype for your customer. Your products or services were created to fill a need for people exactly like you. Thousands of successful companies were started for this reason; Clif Bars, for instance. Clif Bar founder, Gary Erikson, says, "I was a cyclist, I raced bicycles, I owned a bakery, and I worked in the bike industry. And I wanted a better energy bar, for myself."

Erikson started the company because he couldn't stand the taste of the energy bars that were available to him at the time and thought he could make a better product. So he did. And then he went on to make another energy bar designed for women, Luna Bars, which has since become the company's number one selling product. Twenty years later, Erikson still has very strong feelings about his company, its products and its commitments and its philosophy. He passed up an offer of big money along the way from a large public conglomerate, because he cared at least as much about the mission as about personal profit.

Use Your Resources

You can't create successful products or services without understanding and adapting to your customers. This is true no matter what size the company, no matter how big it grows. That's why it's easiest to try and solve a problem you have had yourself. The better you understand the problem, the better your solution is likely to be. The better the solution, the more it will be worth to others. The higher the value to others, and the more of them that there are in the world, the more successful your company will be, both financially and in mindshare.

If you do decide to venture outside of your own realm of experience, you should at least have access to a pool of people to survey – preferably a pool of people that share the problem you're trying to solve. But it might not be enough to just ask them.

Presumably, you have a network of family and friends. So start with the people you know. If you're like me, the people you know and spend time with are diverse in their levels of education, professions, hobbies, viewpoints, values and philosophies. Some are strictly individual consumers and some are business decision-makers that have purchasing power in the millions of dollars.

You know some of these people quite well and could anticipate how they might answer your questions. About others, you haven't a clue, but you know them well enough to ask questions and get honest answers. In some situations, you have the ability to observe their behavior and engage in casual conversations, listening for the particular kinds of clues that will give you insight into their likely interest in products or services. The point is, you probably have more market research resources at your fingertips than you realize.

Talk to People

The whole industry known as market research is built upon simply talking to people – asking about their opinions, their preferences and their habits. The discipline started to take shape in the 1920s as an offshoot of advertising.

During the Golden Age of Radio, advertisers and sponsors began to understand how valuable it would be to have demographic information. They saw that it could be very useful in determining what programs they should sponsor. In other words, they figured out that if the kind of people who had a need for their product regularly tuned in to a certain soap opera, then they should sponsor that certain soap opera. The theory was that listeners would feel loyalty toward the company that brought them their favorite programs.

Market Research Pitfalls

Traditional market research depends heavily on self-reporting, in focus groups or interviews. It relies on the honesty and the objectivity of the very subjects that are being studied. But people aren't always willing to be or even capable of being honest.

Not that they deliberately lie all of the time. It's just that other motives or reactions get in the way. Here are some examples:

- In many focus groups and individual interviews the subject says what he thinks the researcher wants to hear. Or he reports behaving in a way that he believes he should, but rarely does. For example, "I hardly ever watch TV." "I drink one or two beers a week, at most." "I always wash my hands before I touch food."
- Sometimes groups of people feel compelled to agree with or riff on the opinions of one strong and outspoken member of the group.
- People are certainly not objective when the questions are focused on themselves or people they know well.
- People don't always know or can't always tell you what they need. Especially when the "thing" hasn't been invented yet. No focus group in 2002 would have conjured a home thermostat that you could control remotely from your cell phone.

133

"If I had asked people what they wanted, they would have said a faster horse."

Henry Ford

Buy Now Buttons

In the last couple of decades, a newer and potentially more interesting dimension has been added. With the study of neuropsychology, we are gaining a deeper understanding of how the brain works and therefore a deeper understanding of our own behaviors.

This is very exciting and more than a little frightening. Part of me relishes the idea that human beings are so highly evolved, so complex of intellect, that we are forever inscrutable – that our behaviors can never be explained simply by chemistry or any other hard science.

The other part can't wait for the day when we become so predictable that experts in brain science can coach us on how to act and what to say to trigger a desired act – to push our "buy now" buttons – or conversely, to defend ourselves against having them pushed.

Anthropology to the Rescue

Like most aspects of the advertising industry, market research has grown in complexity and nuance with ever more practitioners, segmentation and technological sophistication. To help reconnect with the marketplace, elaborate schemes for gathering intelligence have been devised. And the big brains at universities and business schools ponder the philosophy of needs, not necessarily the needs themselves.

But there's another way. And it owes a lot to Anthropology – which I might happen to know a thing or two about.

Anthropologists have been keeping ethnographic records since the 1920s. In other words, field research – living among primitive cultures and writing down every bit of daily minutiae in hope of recording for posterity and gaining insight or understanding.

There is a lesson to be learned here for product developers, advertisers and communications professionals. Sometimes, it is imperative to step outside of our own lives, biases and priorities in order to understand the needs of others. (Really, you could just think of it like a marriage.)

This observational or ethnographic method can help us create a product or a service that will be useful for people who are not like ourselves. Armed with empirical data, we are more likely to have that a-ha epiphany as we try to design something for someone who has a perspective or a lifestyle very different from our own.

Why Not You?

The customer is better than the Delphic Oracle for business. He or she is the source of wise counsel and prophetic opinion that must be carefully considered. The customer is an infallible authority on whether a product feature matters or doesn't, is worth the price, or isn't.

If you're the Firebrand I think you are, then you've had many moments in your life when you've thought, "someone should create a business to fulfill that unmet need." And then one day, you decide to step into the void and do it yourself.

Perhaps you think that I'm making this sound as easy as pie – when in actuality, there are probably many obstacles to fulfilling unmet needs. Otherwise someone else would already have a successful business meeting this need. That's true. There are always obstacles.

For some vexing problems, the obstacles seem insurmountable. But they never are. They just require someone who refuses to quit trying.

There is always a way. (You can quote me on this.) And someday, someone who doesn't understand the word "no," will find it.

Why not you?

The Cowboy Hat You Don't Know

A hundred years ago, it was John B. Stetson. He was the seventh of a dozen children born to a successful hat maker in East Orange, New Jersey. After living through a series of Lemony Snicket-like unfortunate events, Stetson ultimately founded one of the most enduring brands of the 20th century.

As a kid, Stetson contracted tuberculosis and, fearing an early death, decided to go see the American West. But a funny thing happened: the kid didn't die. Stetson bounced back and wound up in St. Joseph, Missouri in the company of some rough-and-tumble types. Drovers and bushwhackers, or by today's standards, cowboys. And every one of them had something in common.

None of the cowboy's heads were properly covered for the kind of work they did. Stetson saw coonskin caps and derbies and whatnot, but nothing that really protected people from the noonday sun, torrential rain, biting flies or settling dust.

At the age of 35, Stetson moved back east and went into the family business. He opened a shop in Philadelphia and decided to make a hat that would better meet the needs of the cowboy – the hat that became known as the Stetson 'Boss of the Plains.'

Not only did Stetson create a product that didn't exist before, he made sure it had all the attributes his

139

customer needed. But beyond his own observations, how did he know what those were?

Vertical Adaptation

Stetson had great instincts. He was a natural born Firebrand, breaking every rule that had been the industry standard for hat making and marketing up to that time:

- Stetson made it easy for potential customers to see the benefits of his product. While other manufacturers were sending photos and sketches of their tophats and derbies to retailers and expecting customers to order them out of catalogs, Stetson sent free samples and asked the storekeeper to display them.
- Stetson gathered information about what customers wanted. He hired traveling salesmen to call on stores. Naturally, the salesmen got to know the merchants and their customers. They sent back the messages regarding what features were favored and what would be ideal: bigger brims, higher crowns or darker colors.
- Stetson created a nimble organization that allowed him to control his product. He adopted the Henry Ford approach to manufacturing. In an industry that traditionally relied on tiny, hand-crafted, custom shops, Stetson built a factory in Philadelphia, automating as many processes as he could. And he owned the whole supply chain, from manufacturing the machines that

made the hats, to the fabrication of the felt that was the primary raw material of the finished goods.

"Greatness is not a function of circumstance. Greatness, it turns out, is largely a matter of conscious choice, and discipline."

Jim Collins

Relationships

No one is in business in spite of the customer – in fact, you should be in business *because* of the customer. If other people didn't have needs that we could fulfill, we would all still be hunters and gatherers, foraging for ourselves.

Big companies sometimes lose sight of this simple truth. Over time, they forget their roots, growing into complex organizations with lots of layers of management and administration, production and supply chain integration. Most of the people whose livelihoods ultimately depend on the customers are completely out of touch with them. If you surveyed the work force of a very large company, I wonder how many of them would be able to tell you why customers buy or what they most care about.

Treat Customers Like Human Beings

Not long ago, my husband went to the bank and tried to exchange the last of his Canadian money from a recent trip back into U.S. dollars. He pulled out a Canadian five and asked the teller if he could give him the equivalent amount. The teller told him he could only do this for customers of the bank, so my husband revealed that the bank held our home mortgage. The teller looked him up on his computer by his social security number and acknowledged that yes, indeed it was true. Still, since he didn't have a checking or savings account with the bank, my husband wasn't permitted to exchange his five Canadian dollars.

I understand that big companies need policies. In fact, all companies, no matter what size they are, need policies. Ideally, their policies should be an integral part of their brands – reflecting their integrity and how they view their relationships. The front line people in any organization are responsible for following those policies.

But in organizations where policies, applied rigidly, are counter to good customer relationships, a well-trained and savvy customer service representative could have created a positive brand experience instead of a negative one. That teller could have asked a manager for an exception. A really great company representative would have communicated the incident to management at the end of the day

145

and suggested that the policy be reviewed. The front line people don't have to be business geniuses to see this. They don't have to be any more sophisticated than knowing how they would feel if the shoe were on the other foot. Sometimes it's just clear at the point of contact that an organization is really risking nothing to make a customer, with a small and inconsequential request, happy and satisfied instead of annoyed and unappreciated.

When it comes to the service part of industries, it's not that difficult to get it right when you're small. As you grow larger and upper management takes its eye off the "relationships" ball, a brand is in danger of dying a death from a thousand cuts. Many small problems collectively cause a big pain. Or, with a workforce that understands the customer and the value of the relationship and has some latitude in applying policy, it can reinforce the brand and drive customer loyalty.

Be Nimble

Challenger Brands have a huge advantage here. Before rules and regulations get set in stone, companies can vow to remain nimble, even as they grow large. They can set policy that ensures that the entire workforce, in all parts of the organization, remain aware of the vision, the brand and the desired ideal for customer relationships and has the flexibility to act in the company's best interest without sacrificing critical relationships.

Complaints Are Opportunities

Oddly, one of the best avenues for building good customer relationships is in your response to their complaints.

Where there are complaints, there are opportunities. The more complaints there are, especially multiple complaints about the same kind of thing, the better the chance for business success. This is because complaints accomplish two things. First, they give you a clear understanding of what customers really care about. Presumably, people won't take the time or energy to complain about things that don't really matter to them. Second, complaints force you to make a decision about what your brand is going to stand for, what your policy will be and how you're going to shape your future relationships and with which customers.

It might not seem so at first, but this is an important moment in brand development. At these junctures, you are making a statement about your brand. You are saying, "This is who we are, how we behave and with whom we choose to do business." These statements position your brand for future success because they will attract exactly the kind of people you can best serve as customers and they will repel the kind that will waste your time and rip you off track.

In short, when your customers are inclined to give you a spanking, take it like a brand.

Preaching, Practicing

I am very fond of my best clients. My account staff sometimes complains that I "give away the store" because I develop close and often personal relationships with these customers. We spend a lot of time talking about not just business, but also about family, life, money, sex, religion and politics. You know, all the good stuff. If I'm talking to you about the weather, you know we're just in the "getting to know you" stage.

I admit, during business conversations, I am sometimes crossing the line between casual conversation or emotional support and actually consulting and making strategic recommendations. My staff accuses me of giving away not just "swag," but our core product. They point out that maybe a brand strategist shouldn't spend so much time sharing ideas without billing for it.

I can't argue with the facts here. It's true. But I have a different view of the cost/benefit analysis of maintaining such close relationships.

I believe that the benefit my company derives from the time I invest, even considering the non-billable component, far outweighs what I am sacrificing. We learn what matters to the client. We learn about the internal struggles within their organizations to get good ideas accepted and acted upon. We learn about the barriers they face with their customers, their regulators, their competitors and their supply chains.

These conversations not only help us serve them better in the long run, because we come to understand them so well, but they provide us with tremendous insight and value for our other current and future clients. We become very knowledgeable about a wide array of topics. I say "we," because to the extent possible, I share what I learn with my colleagues at Fitting Group and encourage them to follow suit.

In addition, this approach makes my customers feel really good about the relationship they have with me and my company. They feel listened to, respected and most reassuringly, not at all "nickel and dimed." As a result, they often bring up ways in which we can further serve them; hence, we extend the relationship by regularly having the opportunity to sell them more.

Challenger Brands benefit greatly from having close relationships with their customers. This is how they keep their fingers on the pulse of customer needs as well as the competitive landscape without paying for what often turns out to be more expensive and less reliable market research. Challenger Brands still can, and definitely should, take the notion of "voice of customer" quite literally.

Knowing the Customer

Having said all of this about keeping your customer close, a relationship doesn't *always* mean you must personally know each and every one of your customers. In many cases, this is impossible. Good branding could mean that your brand is an important part of your customers' lives or of how they feel about themselves. This is especially the case when it comes to consumer products.

We tend to define ourselves in a multitude of ways, depending on the circumstances at the moment. In that moment, we may associate ourselves with certain brands – the brands that best reflect how we choose to see ourselves. For example, when I'm in the 'Mom' role I'm thinking more about wholesome meals and safe cars and the cellular service that will allow my family to stay in close touch. When I'm in my role as a woman, I want to project a certain image via the clothes I wear or the cosmetics I use. And as a person in a civic and conservation-minded role, I want to associate myself with local and green and sustainable products as much as I can.

When I get to the office, I don the cloak of Brandee, the Brand Spanking dominatrix. This is my brand symbolism – the imagery that I hope communicates to current and future clients what they can expect from me and everyone at my agency: leadership, strategy and creative thinking delivered with a sense of humor that they won't get anywhere else.

151

Two of our favorite clients, with whom we have now had relationships for over seven years each, were each initially attracted to us by our strong branding. They embraced the notion of Challenger thinking. They were amused and stimulated by our imagery. They plainly said they wanted to be pushed and motivated and challenged by us to be authentic, provocative and assertive in their marketing and advertising.

In both cases, however, when it was time for Fitting Group, as a service partner, to peek out from behind our cloaked agency role – like when we wanted to support our clients with a paid sponsorship message in a newspaper or program booklet – they asked us not to feature Brandee, our iconic dominatrix. So as not to offend anyone, you see.

I get it. These are serious leaders who like to think of themselves as intellectual and capable business people. It's not that they don't have a sense of humor, it's that while in the role of Serious CEO, it is incongruous to admit, even by association, that they are amused by a leather-clad dominatrix. They'd rather not have to respond to raised eyebrows. And in this situation, that's ok with me.

People Against Dirty

Creating a brand that becomes one of the ways that people like to define themselves, show off to others and endorse at any opportunity isn't easy. We all joke about our brands 'becoming a household name' but to Adam Lowry and Eric Ryan, founders of Method brand personal and home cleaning products, this is no joke. And if you're a Challenger Brand looking for an idol or two to worship, these are your guys.

These two Firebrands, one a chemical engineer and the other a former ad guy, have been pals since high school. They started their company in 2001, and in a mere nine years, a blink in brand-building terms, Method is a $100 million company and number 16 on *Fast Company's* most innovative companies list.

They won this position for their amazing products, of course, but also as *Fast Company* puts it, for "giving the middle finger to the consumer-products playbook." Lowry and Ryan make ecologically sustainable (read: green) products, but half if not more of their customers don't give a hoot about that. Some of them didn't even realize the products were green. What they love most about Method is the packaging – ersatz works of art that were originally designed by Karim Rashid, the hotshot industrial designer. (Method has now brought packaging design in house.)

153

Customers also like the fragrances within the packaging. And, oh yeah, they kind of like the fact that the stuff works.

From the start, Method didn't just set out to be the best "green" cleaning products. They seemed to have the cleaning product giants like Unilever and Procter & Gamble in their crosshairs from the get go. Any residual doubt that Method was a Challenger in the true sense of the word was finally quelled when the company launched an assault against P & G's blockbuster Swiffer. Method's Omop, a sleek silver reusable mop, employs refill cloths made from corn-based plastic (PLA). Instead of clogging landfills, they're 100% biodegradable.

Adam Morgan (*Eating the Big Fish*) defined Challenger Brands as those companies that change the way consumers view their industry. There is little doubt that Method has changed the way people think and feel about their cleaning products and about the companies that make them. The Method boys have written a book, *Squeaky Green*. I'm not sure I'd be as interested in a book written by the CEO of Procter & Gamble.

The Great Wall

Like every Challenger, Method has often been confronted with the naysayers, the fearful, and the short-sighted. They were not deterred. When every U.S. manufacturer of Swiffer-style cloths told them they couldn't make the product out of PLA, they went to a factory in China that was willing to take on the challenge. That statement alone should strike fear and humility in the hearts of every American who ever complained about outsourcing or the decline of American economic dominance. It may be a foreshadowing of the trends to come for a very long time. And it makes me think that in reality, the "great wall," at least as far as Challengers are concerned, may not be in China at all, but right here in the United States.

So yes, Challenger Brands change the way the world views an industry, and then the market leaders must tear their attention away from quarterly profits and respond to this new perspective if they want to stay alive. The leading cleaning product companies are on it. Just take a walk down the relevant supermarket aisles. SC Johnson acquired The Caldrea Company, which owns Mrs. Meyers brand, in 2008. Clorox has Green Works. Both are wise enough to see the soap scum on the wall.

In an interview with *Fast Company* reporter Danielle Sacks, Method's Eric Ryan summed it up this way: "When we started this company, we had a saying that we were never going to try to out-Clorox Clorox. We shifted the playing field where now companies are trying to out-Method Method."

Couldn't have said it better myself.

"Success is not for the timid. It is
for those who seek guidance,
make decisions, and take decisive
action."

Jose Silva

Growing Pains

The bigger a company grows, the more distance between the founder and subsequent chief executives – that's just the way it goes. Even an original founder with a large organization can't control or reach everyone, so it becomes imperative to establish very, very clear guidelines for the brand and to lead by example.

Psychology is important. Communication skills are important. Passion is important. But the most important thing is that on a daily basis, the brand leader deliberately and consciously instructs, nurtures, encourages, and leads members of the team in delivering on the brand.

Today, like all companies, Challenger companies are asking their employees to do more with less. In the US, many of us work longer hours and have less vacation time than our European counterparts. We are really connected to our work 24/7 through our smart phones and tablets. And no matter how much someone loves his job, he doesn't have total freedom to take a break from it whenever he wants to, even if he's in charge.

So the least we can do for our workforce is to give them a brand experience internally that they can fully embrace and makes them feel good about all the time they are spending to benefit the company. This is a triple win – win for the employee, win for the company and win for the customer, who will benefit from dealing with a better brand ambassador.

Agency Handbook

In an earlier chapter on Guidelines, I told you how my agency brand characteristics came to be and how they affect our hiring practices. Now I'll explain how we institutionalize our brand in the human resources area.

From the time the company had its first employee, we planned for growth and tried to behave like a bigger organization, with a framework sturdy enough to handle expansion. We created an employee handbook. It was pretty standard, including the usual policies and procedures. So we rewrote it. We used language that was a lot more fun, light-hearted and irreverent. We interjected humor wherever it was possible to do so without obscuring meaning. The purpose was not to make light of rules. After all, some of those rules are very important for company and employee alike. And some of those rules are only applicable at times of great distress, such as bereavement policies. We certainly didn't want to make fun of something that would be read by a person who may have lost a family member and was in a state of grief.

But why shouldn't an employee handbook, which is mandatory reading for new employees who then have to sign a document stating that they received and read the handbook, be another opportunity to reinforce the brand and remind a new hire that she is glad she chose to join your organization?

Inwardly facing communications are a very important way to reinforce and institutionalize the brand. They need to come before consumer-facing communications because they help train co-workers in exactly how to communicate with the rest of the world.

Stories: Not Just For Bedtime

One of the best and most lasting ways to drive the brand experience home is by constantly telling stories. At Fitting Group we have monthly staff meetings. The main topic of conversation may change, but there are certain standing features of the meeting that are constant and much anticipated by our team members.

One of these is the "Spanker of the Month" award. Each month team members nominate someone who they believe has performed "above and beyond" the call of duty. All the nominations are read out loud as we try to tie in how what someone has done drives our brand. Then we all vote by secret ballot. The person with the most votes wins. The winner gets to display the trophy on his or her desk for the month. She also gets a cash prize from the company.

The trophy is a toy – Mattel's See N Say – onto which the winner's picture is glued. Those of you who fondly remember this toy know that there are 12 different pre-recorded messages activated by the pull of a lever. The pointer can be turned to a picture and the message plays when the lever is pulled. There are 12 locations that display a co-worker's picture, so we can see a year's worth of Spankers. It brings out the child in all of us and everyone loves to compete for this honor and the cash prize.

Most importantly it is another opportunity to reinforce our brand values. It is easy to see how well the brand is understood when we hear the reasons behind the nominations. Things like breakthrough brand ideas, working long hours to help customers through particularly demanding rebranding efforts and fabulously creative self-promotional campaigns are just a few examples. Also, the See N Say toy itself is symbolic. It is a pop culture icon, another pillar of our brand. At Fitting Group, we believe it is important for all of our team members to stay in touch with pop culture if they are to understand what is meaningful for people on an emotional and evocative level.

Brands, like groups of old friends, have stories to tell and need people to tell them to. When you get together with old friends, don't you find yourself repeating episodes from your past experiences together? If your friends are anything like the groups of friends I know, you do it every time you get together and lots of laughter ensues. When new people join the group, you have to integrate them in by telling all the old stories over and over again.

Brands thrive on this, too. Brands have life breathed into them when lots of members of the tribe repeat their stories to newcomers.

"I have with me two gods, Persuasion and Compulsion."

Themistocles

Emotions and Junk Food

We eat junk food because we're evolved to be attracted to high fat/high sugar foods. This penchant kept us going when we actually *were* on the go and needed all those calories, but we're much more sedentary now. We also eat junk food because it is marketed to us in the most attractive ways – with stimulating colors, with people from central casting and with jingles. In other words, fast food might as well be injected directly into the emotional center of our brains, the amygdala, right alongside drugs, sex and rock and roll.

It is our big brains that have enabled us to figure this out and it is our big brains that have developed the increasingly complex culture that may very well stimulate us intellectually, but starve us physically.

Challengers of every industry should take note. By getting in touch with the emotional triggers of their customers, brands are more likely to strike hard and true with authenticity.

The Power of Triggers

Using triggers in branding, marketing and advertising that set off emotions is the key to making messages memorable and sparking the desire to want to try something.

Certain senses make us remember better. Sounds and smells are extremely powerful triggers.

For some people, the triggers remind them of unimaginable things that cause physical discomfort. Dan Ariely, the behavioral economics guy, was severely burned as a teenager. Here is what he says about his memories:

"Although I can't remember the exact pain I felt during those years, I am also not completely detached from the adversity it brought into my life. When I return for visits to the burn department, when I smell one of the many smells from that period of my life, or even while writing these words now, my state of consciousness changes. There is clearly sadness during these experiences, but there is also a feeling of physical discomfort. I become nauseated, uneasy, my throat dries out. It is hard to fully describe, but somehow my body remembers the emotional residues from that time, and replays them for me."

Imagine if you could trigger the positive version of this physiological response. This is powerful voodoo.

Here Fishy, Fishy

Consider the alligator turtle (*Macrochelys temminckii*). It makes a living by lying completely motionless with its mouth agape, waiting for fish to swim close enough to strike. But chance alone doesn't provide enough food for these guys to become the largest freshwater turtles in North America. They have a trick up their, uh, throats.

At the tip of the alligator turtle's tongue is a wiggly, wormy, red appendage. In essence, a lure. The rest of the turtle's mouth is camouflaged to look like its surroundings, so this bright piece of writhing tongue attracts the attention of fish. Of course, by the time a fish realizes the "worm" is not lunch, the fish has become the meal.

The moral of this fish story is you cannot sit and wait for customers to learn how spectacular your brand is. You need to entice them. You must give them a reason to nibble, to taste, to switch. Once they have, it'll be up to your brand to uphold the promise. But it might never have a chance if you're hiding in the mud at the bottom of a river.

Book 2: Brand Spanking®

Now What?

You've made it this far. This means you 1.) are a Challenger, 2.) believe in the power of branding, 3). know you need to change and 4.) want to know how already!

Good. It's time we turn the speakers up to 11.

"Gold medals aren't really made of gold. They're made of sweat, determination, and a hard-to-find alloy called guts."

Dan Gable, wrestler

Leaders of Challenger Brands

Not every brand that is something other than the market leader is a Challenger Brand.

Challenger Brands require a certain personality, including ambition, confidence and stomach for risk. The leaders of Challenger Brands have to ignore detractors, pessimists and scaredy cats who would talk them out of what they know in their gut is the right thing to do.

These leaders of Challenger Brands are such special people that I believe they deserve their own term. I have named them Firebrands and I've already given you a few examples on earlier pages. This book is really for the likes of them.

Firebrands

The dictionary defines a "firebrand" as a person who kindles strife or encourages unrest, an agitator, a troublemaker.

This is partly why I like the term. Firebrands are people willing to burn down the old to make way for the new, people who spark ideas and new ways of doing things, people who eschew the rules of the category that no longer make sense and institute new ones.

And if you're going to do any of those things, you will undoubtedly agitate those mired in old mindsets and cause strife for those too afraid to take risk or try out new ideas. This is why many firebrands are viewed as unpopular, eccentric or egotistic. These are labels used by fearful and established leaders to smother the embers of innovation.

Firebrands are very much like roaring blazes. They are dangerous and fascinating all at once. And depending on your relationship, they can provide warmth, energy and excitement or they can burn down your house.

No Guarantees

One of the hallmarks of a true Firebrand is the willingness to act, even without guarantees. No. Especially without guarantees.

Those who wait for the sure thing or safety net are clearly not risk takers – and frankly, these folks make terrible entrepreneurs.

Firebrand Neuroscience

If you're still reading this book, it's not an accident. Locked within your genetic code are genes that predispose you to take chances, gamble and come out on top.

Jonah Lehrer titled it "the Wall Street Gene." Others have called it "the Goldilocks Gene" because the people who possess it seem to have just the right levels of dopamine distribution to take risks without losing sight of the long-term.

But you don't have to be a neuroscientist to know what it's like to make decisions based on some gut-feeling that may or may not be lodged beneath your spleen. It's the reason we Firebrands get out of bed in the morning – or more likely, the middle of the night.

Firebrand Personality

Firebrands are willing to expose themselves. Not like exhibitionists, per se. More like the first berserker out of the trenches.

Firebrands are often people who live contrarian lives and don't really care what others think. They don't seek attention for themselves because of ego or a need for personal validation. Instead, they feel that they must champion their cause because no one else will.

Firebrands are able to suspend their fears of ridicule or shame and are willing to sacrifice their privacy. They don't allow repeated failures or disappointment to derail their missions. They focus, laser-like, on a target – whether it's a competitor, traction for an idea or achieving some sort of critical mass of sales for their product or service.

Vision. Ideas. Guts.

Challenger Brands cannot survive without these three elements. Vision is being able to imagine what could be if things were different and also being able to articulate it. Lots of people have vision; not everyone can communicate it.

Ideas are the vehicles by which a Firebrand can drive her company toward that imagined future. Lots of people have ideas. Not all of them are good.

But the most important ingredient for Challenger success is guts. It's also the least common.

Intestinal Fortitude

Anyone can put a plan on paper. Putting that plan into action and taking it all the way is something entirely different. Even the most imaginative vision and the best ideas rarely lead directly to success. There are almost always bumps in the road – setbacks that can deter even the most stalwart among us. But the ultimate Challenger Brand leader knows in her gut that she has it right and doesn't let any naysayer or detractor rip her off course.

Andrea F. Fitting

The Susan G. Komen Foundation

Not all powerful brands represent products and services. Some are created to change the world by changing attitudes.

Nancy Brinker loved her older sister more than anyone else in the world. They were so close all their lives that they never did anything important without discussing it at length with each other. Susan was Nancy's best friend, her alter ego, her fiercest supporter.

And then Nancy found out that Susan was dying of breast cancer. For two and a half years of agony and false hope, going through surgery and chemotherapy and radiation, the sisters held hands. Near the end, through the tears, they made a pact. Nancy agreed to do whatever she could to prevent others from dying of this vicious disease. Then Susan died, leaving behind two young children and a grieving widower. Nancy was still a young woman, with her whole life still in front of her. She felt helpless and guilty for surviving. And she felt determined. She would make certain that her sister did not die in vain. She vowed to do whatever it takes for the rest of her life, if she had to, to eradicate the enemy, breast cancer. This is what launched Nancy Brinker's journey.

Now into her mid-sixties, Nancy Brinker has spent the last three decades building the Susan G. Komen Foundation, a powerful non-profit organization

178

dedicated in her sister's name, to finding the cure. Its signature event, the Race for the Cure, has spread throughout the U.S. and a multitude of other countries and has raised $1.5 billion to fund screening, education and research to fight breast cancer.

Nancy founded the Susan G. Komen Foundation in 1982 and two years later, was herself diagnosed with breast cancer. She underwent four rounds of chemotherapy and a mastectomy, saving her life and perhaps steeling her resolve to expunge the disease.

Nancy has been described as relentless, intense, a bullet. A warrior queen.

I call her a Firebrand.

Challenges & Challengers

This kind of energy and singular focus is common among Challenger Brand leaders. Interestingly, these same people often suffer from learning disabilities.

Those with learning disabilities must work harder in school to keep up and typically fare poorly against conventional methods of competition, such as standardized tests. Perhaps this is why some people forced to blaze their own trails as children tend to continue to innovate and challenge conventional thinking as adults.

In Nancy Brinker's case, the learning challenge was dyslexia. But conditions like dyslexia alone do not explain the intestinal fortitude and drive that propelled Nancy Brinker in the face of some of the failures she encountered along the way.

One story she tells is of a trip to New York to persuade a bra manufacturer's board of directors to put a breast cancer awareness hangtag on their lingerie. In response, they threw her out... literally. Escorted from the building, she stood on the Garment District street corner in Manhattan and cried. This is the type of incident that only further fueled her resolve to change the public's attitude about breast cancer.

Other notable dyslexics include:

- Richard Branson (Virgin)
- Charles Schwab (Charles Schwab)
- Ted Turner (Turner Broadcasting Systems)
- John Chambers (Cisco)
- Henry Ford (Ford Motor Company)

Don't Quit Until Nomads Know Your Name

I was in Israel in 2007 and I witnessed the "power of the pink" with my own eyes. On a beautiful, sunny Sunday in the Karmiel/Misgav region, in the hills overlooking the Galilee, a joint committee of American and Israeli organizers held a Race for the Cure. The parade was preceded by a festival with arts & crafts booths, musicians, and many, many groups wearing brightly colored team shirts and other signature clothing.

One of the groups was notable because of their unusual attire. They wore loose, colorfully embroidered flowing robes that covered them from head to foot. They were Bedouins, Arab women in stunning outfits, milling about, waiting for the march to begin. The small groups were accompanied by a few Bedouin men, hovering around as if protecting their women.

In Bedouin culture, it is unacceptable to acknowledge breast cancer and thus, there is massive resistance against screening mammography. In their belief system, acknowledging that disease is even possible is akin to bringing it on. As a result, many women go undiagnosed or are only identified in the late stages. Sadly, many die from the disease when it could have been treated if detected earlier. So the fact that these women (and their men) were here was a really, really big deal.

182

Against all odds, the powerful messages and dollars of the Susan G. Komen Foundation had reached their remote camps and implored the Bedouin men to save their mothers and wives and daughters. Here was the evidence that it was working. They were talking and singing, basking in the bright sunshine and drinking tea.

It was one of a million small miracles cascading from the passion and boundless energy of one woman still fighting the good fight.

Don't Stop Thinking About Tomorrow

For all the good the Komen Foundation has brought us, no brand is impenetrable.

In 2012, the Komen Foundation decided to stop funding Planned Parenthood because a small portion of its operations were devoted to abortions. And despite where you might fall on the political spectrum, everyone can appreciate the unbridled show of force Komen experienced from its base.

From donors and supporters to the media and Congress, people lost it. The whole pink movement was in jeopardy and every brand that had donned a ribbon or trotted out a product pairing had a stake.

In the end, the Komen Foundation reversed its decision, but the lesson remains: no brand is sacred, no brand is safe. Be vigilant.

"Whenever you see a successful business, someone once made a courageous decision."

Peter Drucker

Take to the Woods

Early on in the American Revolution, our forces found they couldn't match the British in traditional open-field combat. The Redcoats simply had more resources, more firepower and more foot soldiers. After all, they were the greatest empire the world had ever known. Goliath, bar none.

So the Colonials did something that every other army in Europe – in other words, everyone who mattered – considered to be unfashionable.

They took to the woods.

And from the woods, the Revolutionaries waged a war that took away their enemy's advantages. More importantly, it played to their own strengths. And they won.

Play to Your Strengths

Challengers are in a similar situation. The open field has not worked for us. But leaving it presents us with opportunities for innovation. By taking to the woods, we can be:

- Nimble and Agile – reacting to the landscape and adapting to our surroundings
- Accurate – firing from a position we choose, with reliable weapons, at specific demographics
- Unpredictable – slipping between the trees, executing our business in a way the others wouldn't dare
- Resourceful – utilizing the input of our entire team and shaping our organization from within
- Revolutionary – overthrowing the status quo, doing business like it's never been done before

Staring Down the Cannons

We see our competitors' ads and read about their stats. It would be wrong to let them intimidate us and force us to react.

Our enemies are out there with their war machine. They're waiting for us in an open field with bright red uniforms and hulking cannons. Shall we do as others have done and march out to meet them?

Or shall we smear ourselves in war paint, streak through the trees and strike before the break of day?

Differentiate or, Well, You Know

In business, it's important to differentiate. So important, to say so has become trite, a given. Some business marketing gurus like Jack Trout and Steve Rivkin even put it in life-or-death terms, as in their book, *Differentiate or Die*. They and others in the same "club" believe that today's consumers are so overwhelmed with choice that the only way for companies to survive is to make their competitors irrelevant. They give you lots of nuts and bolts ways to accomplish this and use some of the world's best-known brands as examples of both success and failure. These types of books can be quite inspirational and entertaining if the reader already has context or framework within which to place them.

Most business decision-makers usually have at least a vague idea of what differentiation means. But when it comes to understanding the psychology behind why this is so important, many of them have no idea. And even fewer of them have any clue about how to get it done. It is a very rare marketer who grasps that he needs to know how certain people (his desired market) live their lives so that he can shape his product as well as the promotion of it to precisely fulfill their needs and expectations.

Rules, Schmules

Say you're driving down the road and you see a billboard advertisement for a new brand of batteries called TRAQ – invented for this hypothetical – that says, "Our batteries last longer than the leading brand" and you remember, hey, that's right, I need batteries. And when you get to the battery aisle, what do you see?

Energizer, Duracell, a store brand and TRAQ, the one from the billboard. The store brand is cheaper but the other three are virtually the same price. Which do you buy?

Be honest. If you're Bargain Basement Betty, you might go for the low price. If reliability and long-lasting are your top must-haves, how do you choose between the other three?

The Energizer Bunny is an iconic symbol that epitomizes "long-lasting." (Besides, after you got over being annoyed by that cymbals-clashing wind-up toy, he became kind of cute.) You can also probably hear the Duracell branded "3 notes" jingle ringing in your head. What's it going to take to overcome these well-worn pathways in your brain and buy the new brand? Would you do it based on the message you saw, "Lasts longer than the leading brand" – yawn – or would you need something… else?

What if the billboard had featured a sultry woman holding a couple of D batteries with the headline, "Once you go TRAQ, you never go back"?

It's a play on words, a suggestive double entendre and maybe enough personality to buy your one-time allegiance at the checkout counter. (The batteries will have to actually be a good product for you to buy them again, of course, but the trick for Challengers is often about tempting that first brand mutiny.) And if nothing else, this billboard is a mental differentiator of who and what the TRAQ brand is about.

Steel Yourself

Many, dare I say most, marketing directors or CEOs would say "NO WAY!" to an agency that brought them an idea like this. They might be a little more polite about it, especially if they are personally amused and it gives them a feeling of guilty pleasure. In that case, they may say something like "That's clever, but we can't go there. We might offend someone."

And in reality, that's true. People who are puritanical or prudish in their outlook would be offended by an ad that implied something sexual. (Trust me, when I put a dominatrix on our outdoor boards, I heard it all.) Or someone who is always digging deep for a violation of political correctness might even accuse that ad of being racist.

But listen up. Ads should never, ever be created for "the everyman." Ads should be conceived with ONE person in mind. That person is, by demographic profile and definition of lifestyle or behavior, the one most likely to need or want the product being advertised.

So here's one of the places the notion of sacrifice comes into play. In thinking about the target audience and ultimately, the message, we must sacrifice connecting with all other people who have money and decision making power but are unlikely, or at least less likely, to buy what we're selling, no matter how good our advertising ideas are.

In other words, you cannot appeal to all of the people, all of the time. The sooner you embrace this fact and use it to your advantage, the better. Remember this the next time you hear someone say she wants to be "edgy."

A Word on "Edgy"

Many brands claim they want to be "edgy." Of course, what they mean to say is "trendy," "hip" or "with-it." Because for something to be edgy, it needs to be on the *edge* of something. The edge of appropriateness or of good taste. Edgy means nuzzling up against explicitness, vulgarity or politics. It means raising hackles.

When confronted with the true nature of being edgy, many brands run for the hills.

Edgy Isn't for Everyone

But exploring that murky point on the horizon has its benefits for Challengers. Just look at Chris Columbus.

All his life, Columbus pushed boundaries – literally. Some thought he was a fool, others insane. His ideas and courage offended. But today, his name is ubiquitous.

100 Reasons to Say No

There are many, many other reasons marketers shy away from edgy advertising.

They don't think their prospects have a sense of humor. Or maybe they don't really understand their prospects at all. They don't really have the authority to select the ads because the CEO has final say. They are not courageous enough to bet their jobs on good advertising ideas and back down when challenged by executives who know very little about how advertising really works. They fall back on market research in the form of focus groups or other qualitative methods to test creative and then cave-in when one person expresses concern or shock.

Why So Serious?

But the overwhelming reason that marketers turn down creative ideas that are provocative in any way is that they are entirely too serious about their company and its products. They are far too focused internally on things like company rules, politics or power structure. Or they are too focused on the product and its features and not at all on the benefit or value to the customer.

Marketers may truly have themselves convinced that the features of their product are so unique or innovative that people walk around daily thinking to themselves, "If I only had a razor that had 4 blades instead of 3, my life would be exponentially better."

I can assure you, they don't.

A great marketer understands that this is not the way the world works, nor is it the way people think or act. Even the likeliest customer is not thinking about you or your products. He does not automatically make the leap from the way things are in a world with a 3-blade shaver to how much better they would be with a 4-blade shaver. That's because he is not buying a shaver at all. He is buying the possibility of having a smoother face or smoother legs that are a turn-on for his partners. Or he is buying the possibility that he won't have to shave every day. That's why an ad for that 4-blade shaver that focuses on the technological breakthrough of an

197

additional blade is so boring while one that suggests being more attractive to a potential playmate or the ability to skip a day and get away with it, is so much more effective.

It's also why the recent ads by Dollar Shave Club did so well without doing any of the above. (Dollar Shave Club's chief differentiating factor was price point. You could also argue it was their intuition and comedic timing – knowing that people were sick of the add-another-blade-to-your-razor game and were ready to laugh about it.)

An Outsider's Perspective

Truly great marketers have the ability to retain the outsider's perspective – to walk a mile in the shoes of the customer. They have a skill that allows them to step away from what they know about the company, its manufacturing process, its supply chain and its internal politics and put themselves in the head of the one person who has the power to make the company a big success – the ideal customer. This is how they are able to see which messages will work, and which will flop. They can feel the difference in their bones.

Many companies are fortunate enough to have someone with this ability. But many others, especially smaller companies, while they may have numerous talented people with a variety of skills and experience, lack that marketer with the 360-degree perspective.

For those aspiring Challenger Brands, enter the agency, stage left.

The Agency

Yes, Firebrands need help, but what kind of help? Do they need industry subject-matter experts? Do they need seasoned advertising experts? Do they need retired executive mentors?

While these types of counselors might have value, my theory is that the best kind of help for Firebrands is a bit like the equivalent of psychoanalytic counseling or talk therapy. Firebrands need sort of a 'branding coach' – someone who understands the fundamentals of their business, but more importantly, has an uncanny ability to see the brand clearly, speak truth to power and administer some tough love when the Firebrand leader starts to lose momentum or confidence or both.

Good agencies get genuinely and deeply involved in the subject matter of their clients' business without losing that naïveté that enables them to play the role of the customer.

Part cheerleader, part counselor, part mistress or master, and part commissioned artist who sees into the soul of the brand and creates the masterpiece that touches the hearts of the customer audience – that's the role Firebrands need either their Chief Marketing Officer or their agency to play.

"Greatness is not a function of circumstance. Greatness, it turns out, is largely a matter of conscious choice, and discipline."

Jim Collins

Discipline

One of the most important traits a Challenger can have is self-discipline, the kind that makes you focus on the one most important thing in that moment, or on that day, or for that year. The one that will catapult the business to cosmic success.

Of course, it's not that easy. Challengers must, day after day, be compulsive about measuring everything they do against the ultimate goal. Is this activity consistent with what I'm trying to achieve? Will this decision get me one step closer to the goal? If I go off on this tangent what will the impact be on meeting my objectives?

I'm not suggesting that Challengers should be pathological about giving up everything in life for the good of the business. Instead, I believe that Challenger Brands, after taking a break or letting a distraction cause a loss of focus, need to get right back on the horse as soon as possible and start riding it straight to the finish line.

Challengers need to take a tough love approach to anything that dilutes or endangers the brand. Challengers need to sacrifice any ideas or initiatives or opportunities that might yank them off the straightest path to their intended goal.

Rules for Life

In Leo Tolstoy's 10-point manifesto, "Rules for Life,"
the writer offers this sage advice in #5:

"Have a goal for your whole life, a goal for one
section of your life, a goal for a shorter period and a
goal for the year; a goal for every month, a goal for
every week, a goal for every day, a goal for every
hour and for every minute, and sacrifice the lesser
goal to the greater."

Of course, #6 advises us to "stay away from women"
and #1 is to wake at 5 o'clock, so it's not all gold.

But #7?

"Kill desire by work."

Fight the Urge to Fix

This laser-like focus may actually be counter to what comes naturally to a Firebrand. It's the nature of Firebrands to have a multitude of ideas and to solve whatever problems they may encounter in their daily lives.

Firebrands are idea people and the paradox of this is that they are both stubbornly focused no matter what the obstacles and odds and, at the same time, on the journey they are easily distracted by the siren song of other problems or challenges or opportunities. They approach problems by spitting out trial solutions in rapid succession like machine-gun fire. And since it happens so fast, the team is left to sift through a hundred hot and shiny bullet casings, finding it impossible to hold onto any. The good ideas often get away.

And that's the rub.

While wild thinking may be just what Challengers need to get ahead, they don't have the time or resources to create complicated plans with many different strategies, tactics and contingencies.
Moral of the Challenger Brand Story: CBs must sacrifice all other possibilities for the one that is going to propel the brand forward fast — right past the competition — before they even know there is a race.

Strike When the Iron is Hot, and Depressed

Tough economic times make fertile ground for impatient, committed entrepreneurs. The combination of necessity and opportunity and the added dimension of less competition, because so many are daunted by the challenge, have sparked the rise of many wildly successful start-ups. (I mentioned some of them in the first half of this book.)

But not all business successes get their start in troubled economic times. Some Firebrands just give themselves a Spanking when they know they deserve it.

Brian Scudamore, the founder of 1-800-GOT JUNK? did it when his business was already ten years old. At a point in 1998, when he recognized that he had become bored, he made a decision to set new ambitious goals and refuse to let himself fail to reach them.

1-800-GOT-JUNK?

Brian's $1.5 million Vancouver, BC-based junk hauling enterprise was thriving, but it wasn't enough for him. So he made a new plan and wrote it down. That was the key, because he kept referring back to his written plan and feeling anxious if he felt he wasn't making the progress he should be making.

As the title to his plan he wrote 'Top 30 Markets' and he began it with a list of the 30 markets in North America larger than Vancouver that he would need to penetrate to meet his ambitious goals. He described in great detail what the company would look like and how it would be operating five years hence. Then he backtracked and filled in what he would have to accomplish to reach that magnificent goal.

He thought he would have to have 118 dedicated franchisees, all sporting clean, shiny trucks and operated by friendly, clean-cut drivers. As a personal benchmark, he added an appearance on the Oprah Winfrey show to his wish list of objectives.
Brian understood that he couldn't accomplish his dream alone – he would need the buy-in and help of everyone that surrounded him. He would need his tribe. So he began to describe his version of reality to potential franchisees, employees and anyone who would listen. Those who got as excited about the potential as he was would be welcome to help him build the company. But it wasn't just about the goal -

it was the rules of the road that he laid out, that were also of primary importance. Brian focused on the values of the company as well as the financial mile-markers.

Brian was able to bring the plan to life not only because he gave his wholehearted attention to it, but also because the people he surrounded himself with helped propel him forward on the road he had chosen rather than distracting him off onto detours and side streets.

Today, Brian Scudamore, founder and CEO of 1-800-GOT-JUNK?, has turned a venture that started out with one guy and a $700 truck into a $130 million enterprise, now celebrating its 20th anniversary with over 300 franchises in North America and operating in 47 markets around the world.

Monkey Wars & Branding

Deep in the rainforests of Panama, capuchin monkeys live in large groups with overlapping territories. Sometimes, they coexist peacefully. Other times, they wage bloody, territorial battles against their rivals.

For every extra monkey a group has, its odds of victory go up. Might makes right. Right?

Well, not always. Big groups can be unwieldy. One study found that for every additional member in the army, the odds that an individual monkey will desert the cause also went up.

And get this: the battle's context can have a huge effect. "For every 100 metres that they move away from the centre of their territory, their odds of victory fall by 31 percent," says science writer Ed Yong.

In other words, large monkey armies don't do so well far from home. That's why small, dedicated groups of capuchins are able to defend their home bases against the conquering hordes. Though they are few, each monkey knows what he has to fight for.

Plant Your Flag

Businesses make this mistake all the time. They try to capture too much territory – from market positioning and SEO strategy to product offerings – and they wind up losing ground to a smaller, more disciplined brand.

Bigger doesn't always mean better. If the capuchins can pull off an upset, so can your Challenger Brand. To do so, you'll have to remain committed. You must not waiver in the face of uncertainty. And you can't up and change your positioning or products every time your rival puts out a new ad.

Learn your brand's territory. Plant a flag at its center. Then defend it like an army of capuchins is howling down your neck.

209

Customers Reward Sacrifice

When you sacrifice all the things you think you could do, all the services you could perform or all the products you could sell, and concentrate on the one that makes you special, the one you do like no other, your customers reward you with their business and with their referrals. They do that because they believe you are the best at what you do or sell. They believe it to the core of their being and so when they talk about or recommend your company, they do so with passion and honesty. Even when you have to tell customers that you can't perform a service or sell them a product that they would also be willing to buy from you, they are just as likely to respect your focus and your integrity as they are to be slightly miffed that they have to find another supplier for the other things they need.

The great thing about being singularly focused is that it becomes so much more convenient to communicate your message, stay on message, and hone your message. It becomes a self-fulfilling prophecy that you are the leading source for your product or service and so, by default, you must be really, really good at it. Otherwise, how could you stay in business? Right?

"We believe in saying no to thousands of projects so that we can focus on the few that are meaningful to us."

Tim Cook, Apple COO (2009)

Andrea F. Fitting

Consistency Is Our Nature

People have nearly an obsessive desire to be and to act consistently. Once we have made a decision and acted on it, we will feel pressure to respond in ways that justify our earlier decision.

Many famous psychologists have studied and validated our desire for consistency as a central motivator of our behavior. I don't want to oversimplify the discussion too much, but for my purposes here, it's enough to think about how the desire for consistency can play right into thoughts about branding.

Consistency explains some of the phenomenon of stubborn loyalty to brands. It's a valuable tool in a society that has become far too complex. So to help ourselves function, we allow ourselves "brand shortcuts." Once we have bought and/or committed to a brand, we don't have to think – no weighing pros and cons, no more tough decisions, no mental energy expended at all. We know we like Starbucks coffee, so why would we fight the current to try another brand? We are satisfied with ordering our office supplies from Staples, so why would we bother opening a new account anywhere else?

Can you begin to see why Challenger Brands have to do something extraordinary to break this inertia?

Avoiding Overwhelm

Something special happens when people personally put their commitments on paper: they live up to what they have written down. This is very powerful stuff. Just as Brian Scudamore said a few pages earlier – once he put his plan on paper, the fulfillment was much more inevitable.

Consistency plays perhaps an even more important role in our lives than we consciously realize. If instead of acting according to our prior decisions and deeds, we stopped to think through the merits of every new action, we would be overcome and never have time to accomplish anything significant.

What do you think the implications of this are for the Challenger Brand who is running a business that has to be more innovative, more agile and more attractive than the market leader in order to fight the inertia of consumer consistency? Clearly, the Challenger Brand has a tough job.

"Be regular and orderly in your life so that you may be violent and original in your work."

Gustave Flaubert

Breaking Through

The difficulty of breaking through consumer consistency is directly proportional to the risk – to what's at stake. If the product is expensive or a once-in-a lifetime purchase – if it involves a business decision that may put one's job in jeopardy or reflect poorly on a performance appraisal – or if the purchase has life and death consequences – the Challenger Brand will need a whole arsenal of attention-getting and risk-mitigating strategies and tactics to prevail over the market leader.

These strategies and tactics can run the gamut from introducing brand new, never before seen products (think Riedel wine glasses, the first to design the shape of the glass to match the character of the wine) or reinventing a process so that it changes the industry forever (think FedEx, creator of the modern air/ground delivery industry).

The Shotgun Approach

The problem with brands that lack the Challenger ethos, that don't have the firebrand drive or are not confident enough in their brands, is that they try many strategies and tactics at once.

This is the shotgun approach, spreading out resources and hoping that at least one of the strategies will hit the target. Unwilling or unable to focus on one strategy, none of the employed resources can achieve full success.

Challengers need to fight this urge and choose unusual, gutsy strategies. Because doing so requires the most courage, marketers too often shy away. But it's these strategies that are potentially most rewarding, strategies that will truly win them the hearts and minds of customers.

Inbound/Outbound

At least partially, this problem stems from the fact that those responsible for the brand are using an "outbound" rather than "inbound" perspective. They are most likely imagining what form the execution of their brand messaging will take.

Instead, they would be better served by imagining themselves in the shoes of an individual consumer who might buy their product. What is that person worried about today? What need will that person have next week? What process improvement could make that person's life so much easier and more enjoyable? And with potential answers in hand, try to match the ways that they could change their product, their service or their messaging to align with that customer's life.

That's what Brian Scudamore did. He renamed his company 1-800-Got Junk? because he knew that it was the absolute best way to help "unclutter" his customer's mind.

He asked them a question with the solution already in it.

"Here's to the crazy ones. The misfits. The rebels. The trouble-makers. The round pegs in the square holes. The ones who see things differently. They're not fond of rules. And they have no respect for the status-quo. You can quote them. Disagree with them. Glorify, or vilify them. About the only thing you can't do is ignore them. Because they change things. They push the human race forward. And while some may see them as the crazy ones, we see genius. Because the people who are crazy enough to think they can change the world are the ones who do."

Steve Jobs

Full Court Press

David (of Goliath-slaying fame) is the patron saint of Challengers. Many have channeled his storied triumph as motivation for their own brands and I've mentioned him in these pages several times already.

Malcolm Gladwell is also drawn to the underdog parable. In his excellent *New Yorker* piece, "How David Beats Goliath," Gladwell profiles a girls' junior basketball team who achieved major success by employing full-court press during the entire game rather than the traditional last two minutes.

Using a method outside of the accepted norm, these little girls kept pace with teams far more talented, skilled and knowledgeable of the game.

As Gladwell likened it back to the Bible story, "David *pressed*. That's what Davids do when they want to beat Goliaths."

The girls did something unexpected; they chose not to sit back and wait.

And they won. Again and again.

Goliath's Rules

Another interesting point emerges from Gladwell's underdog article. Making use of a database with more than two hundred years of military history between unequal opponents, we learn that Goliath wins only 71.5% of the time. I use the word "only" because this means an army with ten or more times the manpower – those were the metrics for choosing the Goliaths – still loses nearly one-third of the time.

What's more, when the Davids refused to play by Goliath's rules (Gladwell uses the words "unconventional strategy"), their chances of victory increase from 28.5 to 63.6%.

63.6%!

That's more than a fighting chance. That's a likelihood.

War & Branding

Now, we could sit here all day and debate the merits of mixing war and branding metaphors. There's a big difference between business and fighting for your life and isn't it sort of insensitive to draw a moral equivalency between killing a human being and prevailing in business?

Whether you realize it or not, no matter what words you use – your brand is engaged in battle. Your competitors are better funded and better equipped. And to think they aren't plotting your brand's irrelevance and destruction as we speak is to don the fool's mantle.

Lucky for you, a choice exists. You can put this book down and go back to the way you've always done business. I promise, you will not hurt my feelings.

Or – you can chew on those statistics and commit yourself to change your thinking, change your messaging, change your management.

To change.

To risk. To claw. To fight.

To brand with the fury of a thousand suns.

To be a Challenger.

To give yourself a Spanking.

221

Epilogue

"It takes 20 years to be an overnight success."

Eddy Cantor

I Know, I've Been There

I've been working at this business for about a quarter of a century now. I've had my share of glorious, shining moments as well as days spent groveling in the depths of despair. The quote from Eddy Cantor comforts me during the latter.

At one of the lowest points, I doubted my ability to make good decisions and grow the agency. I thought I needed a strong management team of individuals who were expert in their disciplines: creative direction, public relations and strategic planning. After all, weren't these the areas of expertise that a full-service agency required in order to deliver for their clients? So I planned to hire the best minds I could find (and afford) and charge them with plying their skills on behalf of our clients, and on the way, to help create our own brand, too.

I thought that together, we could really build a stronger agency – one that would quickly comprehend the client's problems, understand the big picture, express the client's value proposition and call-to-action through amazing and evocative creative, leverage media and community relations opportunities on the client's behalf and do all of this leading to clear and measurable results the client would love us for.

Oh and one more thing, I wanted to do this all on a daily basis in a friendly, collegial and high-spirited environment. Was that too much to ask? In a word, yes. And in retrospect, it's easy to see why.

First of all, I was hiring for the wrong reasons – fear and self-doubt. Second, I hired the wrong people – again, too weak-minded and eager to get my problems solved – not doing enough due diligence. And third, I was not behaving like a leader (much less a firebrand). No matter how smart and capable other people were, I was indecisive and not communicating what was in my head nearly well enough. In short, I broke all of my own rules.

Needless to say, the outcomes were not as I'd dreamed and I eventually parted ways, one-by-one, with the people on whom I'd hung my hopes. Now I realize that, much like Dorothy in the Land of Oz, I had the solution in my possession the whole time. I just needed to have the confidence in myself and in what was buried in my head – my vision for the agency, my desire to be both conscience and cheerleader for our clients while creating fabulous brand identities, advertising and customer experiences for them and doing all of this while being highly profitable. What's not to love, right?

Fast forward to the present and I'm a different person. I'm no genius, but I am much more perceptive than I ever was. I have the strength of my convictions, ten years more experience and the tough-minded attitude required to tell clients the truth, whether they want to hear it or not. I offer what I think are the right strategies or tactics to solve the problem, based not in small measure on

Andrea F. Fitting

anthropology, behavioral economics and human psychology.

Sure, it's easy to assess now what went wrong back then. But the sheer fact that I'm writing this epilogue means I survived. And with this book, I'm now in a position to help other brands that can't yet see those truths.

Stop Doing Business Like Everyone Else

So it was about ten years ago that we truly began to earn our chops. By necessity, as is the case for many Challengers, we were forced to "Differentiate or Die!"

Standard operating procedure is to market your services to whoever wants them, so long as they are able to pay. Agencies check their mail every day for new requests for proposal (RFPs), lengthy documents rife with legalese and contradiction. "Be creative, but only after we tell you exactly what to do."

Now, it is also SOP for agencies to pour countless man-hours and resources into preparing elaborate pitches in hopes of seducing prospects. There are books written about how to pitch, suggesting theatrics, staging and other over the top antics. And now, to glorify the ridiculous, there is even a reality TV show called *The Pitch*.

Investing time and energy in proposals and intricate presentations to go with them was sucking energy and money out of our business – and the return on investment was not impressive. In fact, many companies that issue RFPs have chosen their provider in advance of the exercise and are just covering their tracks.

So I finally said, "No more."

Guts – you won't get far in this business without them. And I found mine that day. From then on, we would differentiate our brand by what we would *not* do. I think Bill Cosby got it right when he said, "I don't know the key to success, but the key to failure is trying to please everybody."

So, no more responding to RFPs with lengthy proposals, which could take days to write. No more spec work, which demanded huge amounts of time and talent from our whole team. And no more beauty contest presentations where we strut our stuff in front of people who sometimes have made up their minds long before we ever got there, have little point of reference to judge our ideas, or are not even really engaged or particularly interested in the process. Those days are dead and gone.

So, What Do We Do?

To replace the BS of RFPs, I pieced together a brand new approach. We would have a multiple-day "brand therapy" session with the client's management team and the agency team. They would bring all of the key decision makers plus a couple of other representatives – one of their frontline people, the kind who dealt with their customers every day and had special insight, and one of their operations people, the kind who saw the inefficiencies in the system, but didn't feel empowered to point out how to do things better.

We would take the group through a series of directed exercises, facilitating creative thinking by letting go of all the barriers, boundaries and fears that normally hold people back from exploring new possibilities. We would record all of the discussions and ideas, without judgment, and later filter them for what we thought were the best seeds of truth. Then we would add research and information pulled in from other resources to address some of the issues that were raised in the workshop.

Finally, we would make a list of prioritized recommendations and flesh each one out with details, timelines and preliminary budgets.

The result would be a well-thought out document describing the client's current and future branding,

229

positioning, strategy and tactics. In other words, a kickass launch pad for an actionable marketing plan.

Tough sell, right? Still, you can't underestimate a company committed to the 'this-is-the-way-we've-always-done-RFPs' mentality. So we positioned the new approach as a low-risk alternative to choosing an agency the old-fashioned way. We asked them, "What if you could see your company in a whole new light? What if you could do it in two days?" We promised a process that would be eye-opening, energizing and fun.

- There would be brainstorming
- There would be breakthrough insights
- There would be fresh strategies and tactics
- There would be bagels, sandwiches and cocktail shrimp

And in the end, the client would acquire an agency partner that clearly understood them and the dynamics of their management team – a process which under normal circumstances could take up to a full year of doing business together.

At the end of two days, we delivered a formal presentation of the findings and our recommendations for next steps. If the client still liked us and liked the way we thought and interacted with them, they could choose to engage us in executing the plan.

This is how the Brand Spanking Workshop was born.

Encouraging Words

Are you worried about what happens after you close this book? Do you require more than a kick in the ass in paragraph form? Do you need help applying the tenets of Brand Spanking to your would-be Challenger Brand enterprise?

Well you're in luck, sugar. Because I'm willing to be one of your cheerleaders.

Give yourself a Spanking and I'll whisper encouraging words into your ear.

Remember, being a Challenger Brand is more than simply being #2. It's a way of life, an ethos. An oath. Challengers think differently, take risks, navigate by their guts and deface the rules written by their competitors.

If you're ready to stop marching directly into your rival's cannons, I'm here to be your sounding board, your wing man, your kaishaku.

Just say the word.
You can find me at afitting@fittingroup.com

Andrea F. Fitting

Notes

Acknowledgements

I stand on the shoulders of giants. You know who you are. I also owe a debt of gratitude to many who could never imagine that they helped me write this book.

To all of those who actively aided and abetted, thank you.

Several particular shout-outs go to Belinda Yeager Carter and Travis Norris for continued encouragement, Bonnie Budzowski for coaching, reading and mentoring, Krishna Pendyala for support beyond measure, and Debra Dion Krischke for supplying the final kick in the pants...the deadline!

Andrea F. Fitting

About the Author
and her favorite aide de camp

 Andrea Fitting is a brand philosopher, Fulbright Scholar and not-quite-five-foot rouser of rabble. She has been the owner of Fitting Group, a Challenger Brand Agency, since 1986.

Andrea was born in Budapest, Hungary and became a refugee during the Hungarian Revolution. As a result, she has always been a bit of a Challenger Brand herself. In a past iteration of her career, she earned a Ph.D. in Archaeology and Anthropology, wielding a trowel, a plumb bob and a pick mattock with the best of them. Andrea has taught intrepid students of past cultures, traveled extensively to interesting places and loves to eat exotic food. If you find tortured phrases or wording in this book, just remember, English is Andrea's second language.

Jason Bittel holds an MFA in Nonfiction Writing. Jason worked tirelessly to keep Andrea's thoughts coherent and fun to read.

When he's not Brand Spanking as a copywriter at Fitting Group, he writes about weird stuff like opossums at BittelMeThis.com.